It Happened In Brewood

By the same author:

Coven In Times Past

Crime & Chaos In Victorian Penkridge

Tales From Four Towns - Death, Destruction, Crime and Notable News from 19th Century Walsall, Wednesbury, West Bromwich and Wolverhampton

The Rise, Fall and Redemption of James Fairweather

It Happened In Brewood

Paul Robinson

Penk Publishing

Copyright © by Paul Robinson 2016

All Rights Reserved. This book or any portion thereof may not be reproduced or used in any manner whatsoever without the express written permission of the publisher.

Paul Robinson has asserted his right under the Copyright, Designs and Patents Act, 1988, to be identified as the author of this work.

ISBN 978-1-326-55041-7
Penk Publishing
Email: penk.publishing@gmail.com

Contents

Introduction	7
Chapter 1 - Entertainment	9
Chapter 2 - Accidents & Escapes	21
Chapter 3 - Damage, Cruelty & Theft	41
Chapter 4 - Crimes Against The Person	65
Chapter 5 - Pubs & Drink	85
Chapter 6 - Shops, Property, Workhouse & Health	109
References	129

Introduction

While the history and topography of Brewood has been covered in detail by a number of books, and reminiscences from the 20th century have also been gathered together and published, little has been put into print about events in the lives of ordinary people before that century.

Using newspaper reports, censuses and other records, we can get a feel for not just the place in which people lived but what they actually did (or what others did to them!) and what their lives were actually *like*, sometimes even in their own words.

We can find out about their living conditions, what they ate, how they were entertained, what work they did and what happened when things went wrong, whether as a result of accident, disease or crime. This is the focus of 'It Happened In Brewood' - not so much the buildings, the landscape or the 'notable families' of the area, although some of these are mentioned, but events in the lives of ordinary people.

Today, Brewood is usually described as a village but to residents of the nineteenth century it was a town. A much smaller place than Wolverhampton or Stafford, or even

Cannock or Penkridge, but a town nevertheless. As the century progressed and those other places increased in size, Brewood, away from main roads, centres of industry and especially the railway, began to dwindle.

When discussing events of the past, money frequently enters the equation, especially in relation to matters of property and crime. So, for those too young to remember the old 'imperial' system of currency, it will help to know that money was specified in pounds, shillings and pence; there were twelve pence to a shilling and twenty shillings to a pound. Shillings and pence are sometimes abbreviated to 's' and 'd' in the text, for example, 7s 6d being seven shillings and six pence (or "seven and six" as people said at the time). The present day pound symbol has also been used, rather than the 'L' that denoted this value at the time.

Calculating the relative value of money in the past is difficult, but for the century or so covered by this book, one pound was a significant amount of money to the vast majority of the population. Wages were often in pence or shillings per week and many items of food and drink cost just a penny or two - a pound would buy well over 100 pints of ale!

The content of some advertisements, and the words of some individuals have been quoted verbatim in places – punctuation and some spelling may therefore be a little different to what is usually encountered today.

Chapter 1
Entertainment

Brewood Races

An annual horse-racing event was held at Brewood for about twenty five years, beginning in 1834. The racecourse was laid out on land near to Hockerhill Farm, with most races being between one and two miles in length and prize money ranging from one to twenty or more sovereigns, with some races being decided by the overall score after three heats. The influx of visitors must have been a very welcome boost for local businesses, as well as providing entertainment for residents and a degree of civic prestige.

When the event was newly established, the Wolverhampton Chronicle offered its opinion of the course:

> *"We cannot too highly praise the arrangements of the Committee; they have succeeded in an incredibly short period in laying out and forming as pretty a course as any in the kingdom. The*

> horses in running may be seen the whole of the distance from the neighbourhood of the chair; and from these circumstances and the spirit displayed in the neighbourhood, we have little doubt that in another year Brewood Races will take a very respectable station in the sporting world"

At this time, Walter Giffard was the Steward, and the 'Steward's Ordinary' - a lavish meal for the great and good - was held afterwards at 'The Lion', as seems to have been the case for most meetings. At one meeting in September 1837, the feast laid on by Mrs Day was described as "a sumptuous and plentiful display of all that could satisfy the gourmand or tempt the epicure".

The race organisers no doubt tried to pitch the event as a cut above other race meetings, where crime in the form of pick-pocketing, illegal gambling and drunkenness were often encountered. In the early years, the event was said by the Wolverhampton Chronicle to be "attended by a large and respectable company, desirous of enjoying the pleasures of the turf free from the inconveniences which too frequently intermingle with them when their locality is nearer to populous neighbourhoods"!

In 1836 the races were said to be rapidly gaining celebrity, but the advent of railways, the invention of the electric telegraph and the publication of newspapers such as the Sporting Life put paid to any further expansion; people soon had easy access to all the major racecourses, rather than having to struggle to out-of-the-way venues such as Brewood, and results were conveyed to punters across the nation as they happened.

Nevertheless, Brewood Races continued to attract fairly large crowds as well as being patronised by well-known members of the local community in their capacity as owners, riders, sponsors and spectators.

In 1839, the Staffordshire Advertiser was as effusive in its praise as the Chronicle when it trailed the forthcoming event:

> "We always hail the return of these races with high satisfaction. Good sport and good company invariably attend them, and of course the diffuse enjoyment of a kind only to be found where the racing is of the best character and the spectators select. The meeting is, to use an expressive term, the most 'aristocratic' as well as the most friendly little affair in the neighbourhood."

Even at its peak, Brewood Races did not always attract sufficient runners to enable every race to take place - in autumn 1847 for example, one race had too few horses and instead the crowd were treated to a race between cows from local farms! According to the Staffordshire Advertiser it was:

> "a scramble between five 'terrible high-bred cattle' who, though anonymous (at least to us), furnished good sport to all except the owners of the hurdles which were smashed awfully by some of the bunglers".

After this particular meeting, the 'Ordinary' was said by the paper to have been "right merrie"!

As well as racing on the course, steeple-chases were organised at and around the venue, by the Albrighton Hunt. A typical race was run in January 1852, with Henry Wright of The Lion as the Clerk of the Course. It consisted of two laps, totalling three and a half miles, starting at the southern end of the racecourse and passing through freshly ploughed fields, fallow land and an acre of turnips. Considering that each circuit also included thirteen jumps, it is perhaps surprising that eight of the twelve starters made it home; the prize money of 40 sovereigns must have added considerable encouragement.

Steeple-chasing did not take place for two years from 1856 but when it resumed, the races were said to be better patronised than ever. The Wolverhampton Chronicle described the scene, when racing re-started in the spring of 1858:

> *"The weather, often so capricious in the month of March, was splendid: the sky cloudless and serene - the air mild and balmy as in early autumn. The ground was firm and dry and the course in capital condition. Viewed from the neighbourhood of the Judge's chair, at the most elevated point of the ground, and commanding the entire course as well as a pleasant prospect over an extensive tract of country, the scene was most inspiring, particularly for a short time before the principal race came off. At that time the 'grand stand', carpeted with natures covering of verdant green and canopied by a clear blue sky, was thronged by a gay and animated company - some on horseback, many in carriages and more afoot."*

The newspaper made great play of the fact that the event was growing in importance because it promoted some of the "vigour and prowess manifested in past ages" and that professional horse-racing and its pretentious meetings were in decline! A decade or so beforehand, the event had actually been referred to in print as the "Wolverhampton and Brewood Aristocratic Steeple Chase".

One of the later race meetings, held on Monday September 26th 1859, consisted of just three races, the last being for non-thoroughbred horses owned by farmers living within 10 miles of the village. Brooke Chambley of Coven Lawn administered the event, taking stakes and entry fees in advance at the Angel Inn and paying out winnings during the 'Ordinary' at the Lion. Admission to the course was charged at 1d for spectators, 1s for a saddled horse, 1s 6d for a gig and 2s for a coach.

By the start of the next decade the races seem to have petered out completely but steeple-chasing continued; for example in 1860 under the stewardship of Mr Chambley and Captain Fowler of Pendeford, and again with the support of the Albrighton Hunt, a steeple-chase was held at the track and adjacent land.

Weddings, Shows and Sports

The Coronation of Queen Victoria in 1838 was marked by celebrations across the land and in Brewood, according to one report, "...this little town was most conspicuous in its loyal rejoicing".

Almost all houses were decorated with flowers and flags, and wreathes were hung across every street. Proceedings commenced at 11.30am, with a band leading a huge procession, including some 500 children who had been given coronation medals, to the church. After an address by Reverend Haden, the procession was joined by hundreds more people and made its way to Market Place. Some 800 inhabitants, principally men, dined in a specially erected 'room' (presumably a canvas strung above Market Place) while many hundreds more were seated outside. The fare included as much beef, bread and Staffordshire ale as any man wanted to eat or drink. The toast proposed by the vicar was heard in total silence but the response from the assembled crowd was said to be utterly deafening.

Arrangements had been made to accommodate the women and children, of which there were around 1,000, in a nearby field. While they were treated to cake and wine, sixty members of the gentry enjoyed their meal a little later at the Lion Inn. Dinner parties were held at several other local hostelries and the day was rounded off by a dance held at the National School.

Royal events of all kinds were keenly celebrated during Victoria's reign and the wedding between Victoria's son Albert Edward, the Prince of Wales, and Princess Alexandra of Denmark in March 1863 was no exception. Generous donations from individuals of every station meant that the parishioners of Brewood enjoyed a day of celebration that would live in their memories for many years.

Following a church service at 11am, some 900 people were treated to roast beef and plum pudding, while around 500 children enjoyed tea and cake. Food was even delivered to the homes of those who were unable to attend due to illness or infirmity.

For members of the organising committee and the principal inhabitants of the area, the afternoon's entertainment consisted of a meal at the Giffard's Arms followed by a concert performed by local amateur musicians at the school. For everyone else, there was an afternoon of sports held in a nearby field, followed by dancing to the band of Captain Loveridge's Volunteer Company at the Institute.

Working men of the area pooled their resources and bought a sheep, which was roasted whole at the Angel, where a large union flag flew proudly atop and banners draped from the windows declared best wishes for the royal couple. There was a procession through the village at 4pm, led by two horsemen and a brass band. The roasted sheep was carried aloft amidst the parade, decorated with blue ribbons and laurels. Following this second hearty meal, there was a long series of speeches and toasts with music between, followed by a dance which lasted until morning.

In addition to royal weddings, major events in the lives of notable families were often a chance for those of any social standing to enjoy free entertainment. In November 1850 for example, Mr Giffard's niece, Charlotte Simpson, married Thomas Tillotson of York at Brewood church. According to newspaper reports, the wedding was enthusiastically welcomed by locals:

> "The lovely and amiable bride was attired in a beautiful dress of Honiton lace, attended by six

bridesmaids, and given away by her uncle, the popular 'Squire of Chillington'. Every demonstration of respect was shown by the inhabitants of Brewood. Arches of evergreens were erected. The children of the National School strewed flowers on the path, and the church was crowded by the respectable inhabitants of the neighbourhood; but more than all, the warm feelings of the humbler class bespoke the universal respect in which the bride was held, and the sincere good wishes of all for her happiness."

Sometimes however, the wealthier inhabitants of Brewood enjoyed regular entertainment from which those of a lower station were excluded. For example, a dance was held at the Lion Inn and Giffard's Arms in 1849. The event was advertised as a "Select Ball, under the patronage of several families of distinction". The master of ceremonies was Mr Hill, "Professor of Dancing"!

On Friday 19th February 1886, a ball was held at the Old Reading Room in aid of the local soup kitchen, which was much in demand at that time due to a nationwide depression in agriculture. Dancing to a string band continued until the early hours of Saturday morning and guests included Mrs Monckton of Bargate House and Arthur Monckton of Stretton Hall. The Lichfield Mercury reported that a varied programme of music was provided, "so that the most fastidious tripper of the 'light fantastic toe' could hardly complain" and that "the monotonous serenity of this town was somewhat pleasantly relieved".

Some cultural events were open to anyone who was interested, provided they could afford the asking price. One such event was an amateur concert of music, held at the National School under the patronage of the Moncktons and Giffards in June 1865. Tickets ranged in price from sixpence to two shillings and could be had from Charles Green, the chemist, or Henry Burslem, the draper, on Market Place.

Henry Phillips, billed as 'the celebrated vocalist', gave a concert at Brewood 'News Room' (perhaps the reading room?) on 15th February 1859. Seats were charged at two shillings at the front, one at the back and half price for children.

The last Ivetsey Bank Agricultural and Sports show of the century was held in June 1899 in a field near the village. A brass band from Cheslyn Hay provided the music and Arthur Lowder of the Swan Inn supplied the refreshments. Despite being rather wet and misty, around 1,500 people turned out to see competitions for livestock, 'horse-leaping' (ie gymkhana), fence-making, the Fire Brigade's smartest man, tent-pegging and sprinting!

The annual School Sports also attracted a large number of spectators, as they do unto this day, but being a Grammar School they were taken much more seriously. A typical event in 1869 was reported over a couple of column inches in the Birmingham Gazette. The piece included times and distances for the various events, although they were said to be very bad due to the very heavy nature of the turf following recent heavy rain.

The Grammar School's Speech Day was an equally serious annual event; in 1867 it warranted a whole column in the

Staffordshire Advertiser, no doubt due to the attendance of the Earl of Dartmouth, Lord Hatherton and other notable figures.

Prize-fighting was not confined to the towns typically associated with the 'sport'. There are numerous instances of fights with many spectators near Four Ashes, Penkridge, Calf Heath and so on, and doubtless some were held around Brewood. One such took place in 1843, the combatants being George Pershouse and Thomas Beddard and a 'second' to one of the men, Joseph Kenrick. The fight was discovered by police and the three were bound over by Wolverhampton Police Court.

The ordinary man could enjoy many of the same sports and hobbies as he does today. Athletic events, fishing, bird-keeping, shooting competitions, flower and vegetable cultivation were all popular, while horse-racing and later football were favourite spectator sports.

Recreational fishing was as popular in the past as it is today, and owners were just as careful in protecting their stocks. In 1847, Samuel Mills was fined a shilling for fishing in the canal at Brewood and in 1854, a boatman, Robert Smith was fined the same. John Spencer, who was collared by a Chillington gamekeeper, was fined a much stiffer £2 but he had been fishing in the canal with a net rather than a rod.

There were several different gardening societies available in Brewood, to occupy those who were interested in growing or showing. The Brewood Cottage Garden society existed before the middle of the century, with Messrs Giffard and Monckton as President and Vice-President respectively. The society seems to have held three summer shows per year and charged non-members 6d entry. The Brewood and District Horticultural Society was founded in 1852 to meet the needs of keen amateur gardeners but flower arranging was also popular at that time; local vicar Reverend Rushton won a prize for his efforts at Wolverhampton Flower Show in the following year.

Chapter 2
Accidents & Escapes

Fire

By the end of the nineteenth century, fire-fighting, like policing and many other public services, was under the control of local government with many hundreds of municipal brigades offering an ever-improving service, with wider and more responsive coverage. At the start of the Victorian era however, things were very different; most fire engines and firemen were funded by parish councils or insurance companies, with facilities in rural locations usually being extremely limited.

The Brewood fire engine belonged to the Birmingham Fire office, established in 1805. As well as engines in the larger towns of southern Staffordshire, they also had engines stationed at Penkridge, Eccleshall and Stone. The engines were provided to fight fires only at those properties who had fire insurance (and were displaying the appropriate 'fire mark' as proof), although larger estates such as Chillington and Somerford also had their own engines. The fire insurance companies regularly advertised in the local press, often including testimonials from well-known individuals in the area who had found it necessary to call out a fire engine. The cost of annual fire insurance ranged from a few shillings to a hundred pounds or more for the largest properties.

Around the middle of the century, stockbroker John Hay of Dean Street acted as the company's agent in Brewood, while William Mein of 27 Stafford Street was the local agent for London Assurance, who offered both fire and life insurance.

Given the primitive equipment available, firemen would do their best to save lives and contain the blaze, but there was often little choice but to allow a fire to burn itself out. Villagers would also come out to help fight fires during day or night, not just through a sense of community spirit, but because their livelihood might directly or indirectly depend upon it.

With houses reliant upon open fires, candles and lanterns for heat and light, and with little to help in the way of fire prevention, it is unsurprising that naked flames were a constant source of mishap in the past, whether directly or through the insidious effects of carbon monoxide. That said, there are comparatively few reports of serious fires in Brewood during the 1800s – its mostly rural aspect certainly being less likely to suffer the fires that afflicted densely populated and industrialised towns.

On Saturday 13th March 1830, a fire broke out at Park Cottage on the Coven Road. The blaze, which was believed to have been started by an ember from the kitchen chimney, defeated all attempts to bring it under control. The roof was completely destroyed and upper parts of the building badly damaged. The occupant at the time was Mr Careless!

At the start of December 1848, an inquest upon the body of four-year-old George Rhodes was held at the Admiral Rodney. The inquest heard that on the previous Friday, Mrs Rhodes had left the boy eating his dinner while she took a meal to her other son, who was working a couple of hundred yards from their home. She returned just a minute or so later to find the boy's cotton smock ablaze and, despite throwing him into a water-filled ditch, she was too late to save his life. It was thought that a cinder from the fire was to blame and a verdict of "accidental death" was returned.

Almost exactly twelve months later, someone at the opposite end of the age scale, Elizabeth Brotherton, a 70-year-old who lived in a cottage on the edge of Blymhill Common died after falling from her chair onto the fire.

On a Sunday night in spring 1863, 16-year-old Ellen Ward's clothes were set alight by a bedroom candle at her home in Kiddemore Green; she succumbed to her injuries the following morning.

A thatched cottage at Horsebrook was completely destroyed by fire in 1858, but the other five properties in the row were not affected. The fire broke out at around 4pm on a Friday in February, when sparks from the chimney ignited the thatch. The Brewood fire engine was called for, but before it arrived two constables and a number of other people were able to remove all the goods from the house. Buckets of water were thrown onto the roof but even when the engine finally arrived it proved impossible to put out the burning thatch which eventually collapsed. As the burning mass was now within the building, it proved easier to contain and was soon brought under control.

Even wealthier houses were not immune to fire, for they relied upon exactly the same means of heating and lighting as the poorest homes. A fire took hold in the laundry at Somerford Hall in the summer of 1868, completely destroying both laundry and wash-house, despite the Brewood fire engine and the estate's own engine being pressed into service. How the fire started could not be discovered as there was no open fire in the room and none of the servants would admit to taking a light into the place.

In recent years there have been a number of reported attacks on emergency services personnel and their vehicles, when called to deal with fires or accidents, but it seems this is nothing new. In 1860 the Chillington estate fire engine attended a conflagration in Brewood and while it was there, two brothers, Leonard and Charles Waltho, challenged one of the engine crew to a fight. When Edward Tomkinson told Leonard Waltho he was not interested in fighting him, Waltho said his brother would fight him instead. Tomkinson was a gamekeeper on the estate and had obviously encountered the pair before because Charles Waltho then said "You are a *** keeper, and I am a *** poacher, just stand before me". Charles Waltho then lashed out at Tomkinson and his brother attacked Samuel Cliff, another of Mr Giffard's tenants, who was also manning the engine.

When the matter was brought before Wolverhampton Police Court, the defendants called two witnesses who supported their version of events but a policeman who was present backed up the claims of the firemen. The Waltho brothers were found guilty and fined 2s 6d each plus costs.

Transport

For most of the nineteenth century, as in innumerable centuries beforehand, horses supplied the sole means of travelling or moving goods by road as well as providing the power for agriculture and the canal system. There were thought to be over three million horses in Victorian Britain, or roughly one horse for every ten people.

Towns and cities were crowded with horse-drawn vehicles, moving passengers and all manner of goods, between businesses, consumers and the railways and canals. The same variety of vehicles would be seen in lower numbers in small towns and villages. Standing in Market Place in Brewood, an observer would have seen the coal man, baker, grocer and milkman delivering to their customers, the drayman bringing beer to the public houses and carriages conveying passengers to and from the station at Four Ashes. Carts carrying items to and from the many local farms and vehicles moving people and materials to and from Wolverhampton and other places would complete the scene.

With the introduction of the bicycle, motor car and motorcycle, there were new offences for the police and courts to deal with, although most, such as failure to obtain a licence, missing lights, dangerous driving and so on, all had their equivalents in the horse-drawn era.

It is surprising, given the comparatively low speed, how many people met their end by being run over or crushed by their own horse and cart. Many of these accidents were as a result of the 'driver' (walking beside the cart) losing his footing and ending up under the wheels rather than being thrown from the vehicle. A case in point was George Field of Brewood, who was run over by his own cart in March 1841.

George Underwood of Oak Street, Wolverhampton worked at a gas-fittings factory in the town. He and three of his workmates took a horse-drawn cart to Brewood Wakes in September 1864 and while there became completely drunk. As they were passing the Golden Ball at Coven Heath on their way home, the cart overturned and Underwood received such dreadful head injuries that he died shortly afterwards.

Riding on the shafts of a cart, rather than walking beside it, was a dangerous pursuit as well as being a highway offence. Thomas Allsopp, a 36-year-old wagoner of Somerford, was fined 5 shillings plus costs for doing so at Brewood in May 1864.

According to the Staffordshire Advertiser, Darlaston man John Hanford was fined 10s for furiously driving a horse and light cart through the streets of Brewood in July 1864, "thereby endangering the lives and limbs of passengers". No information is provided about who the passengers were or whether it was they who brought the charge.

John Whitehouse of Brewood was also charged with "furious driving" when he appeared at Wolverhampton Police Court in 1872. He was said to have been driving his trap at 7 mph along Stafford Street in Wolverhampton, when there was a collision between his vehicle and that of cabman Richard Barber near the junction with Canal Street. The shaft of Whitehouse's trap pierced the shoulder of the other man's horse and the injury was so severe that it proved fatal. The Magistrate decided that 7mph was not an excessive speed and dismissed the case, while warning all parties to take care when using such busy thoroughfares.

Cannock surgeon Mr Fry suffered a nasty accident when returning home from Brewood in the summer of 1840. The pony drawing his small carriage took fright and he was pitched from the vehicle, breaking both legs and fracturing his hip. It was doubly unfortunate as the poor man had previously been thrown from his horse and suffered a broken thigh which left him unable to ride.

As well as being involved in accidents, carts, or rather their owners, were frequently in trouble for lesser highway offences. In February 1888, Constable Hill noticed an unattended horse and cart on Stafford Street and he sent Constable Lawton to keep an eye on it, believing that the owner was in a public house. When Wolverhampton drayman David Rostin retuned to his vehicle almost an hour later, he was charged with causing an obstruction. Cannock Police court imposed a one shilling fine but added over thirteen shillings in costs.

A quarter of a century earlier, Codsall men John Ralphs and Alexander Meredith committed a different highway offence and both were fined 20 shillings plus costs as a result. They were each drawing two carts 'in train', without one being fastened to the other as the law required.

The case was brought on the recommendation of an inquest jury, after a child name Chetter was killed by one of the carts in question at Weston Heath. Even considering the value of money at that time, the fine seems very slight when their actions were a contributory factor in someone's death – near the end of the century, farmer Vernon Brown of Belfields was fined 25 shillings just for keeping a carriage without a licence.

Road and rail vehicles were not the only form of transport subjected to legislation; canal boats were also regulated, especially after a series of Acts passed in the years either side of 1880. These laws were an attempt to improve the living standards of those working on the canals and required boats to be registered with a local authority. They were then given a numbered certificate and sometimes also had the details painted on the side of the boat. William Tyler, who lived and worked on his narrow-boat, was fined over £1 including costs for failing to produce his certificate when required to do so by the Inspector at Brewood.

Drowning

Little Jane Preston drowned in the canal near Skew Bridge (or Eskew Bridge as it was sometimes known) in November 1847. Six years later, 7 year-old Benjamin Ward and his elder brother were messing about near School Bridge during the summer when the younger child fell into the water. His brother shouted for help and Samuel Large, a chimney sweep who was fishing nearby, immediately leapt into the water to attempt a rescue. Sadly, by the time Mr Large managed to find the boy's body at the bottom of the canal, which was about five feet deep at the spot, it was completely bereft of life. The jury returned a verdict of 'found drowned'.

In January 1861 word spread rapidly around Newport that 35 natives of that place had drowned at Brewood. It was said that some 200 people had gone to Brewood to skate on the frozen reservoir and that the fatalities occurred when the ice gave way beneath them. Friends and relatives were much relieved to learn that the story was completely without foundation. Three years later, an eleven-year-old boy by the name of Ward did fall through the ice on the reservoir. Fortunately using his hands and chin, he was able to cling on until he was rescued a few minutes later.

Taking risks on the ice in pursuit of pleasure was not confined to youngsters, the daring or those of lower intellect - on the very same day as the supposed tragedy at the reservoir, the Coven vicar, Reverend Monckton, fell over while skating on Somerford Pool and suffered concussion. He was unable to conduct services for over a week.

In May 1864, the body of Thomas Ralph, a Wolverhampton coal miner, was found in one of the pools at Chillington. The man had been to a christening at Brewood on a Sunday and, when he left the celebrations at 2 am on Monday morning, was very drunk.

In 1908, local postman George Edward Kirkland was declared a hero for rescuing a little girl from certain death. The child had fallen into a dangerous marl-pit which lay beside Kiddemore Green Road, the mud in the pit being several feet deep. The girl had sunk once and managed to resurface at which point Kirkland, who lived nearby, was alerted and threw himself into the mud to effect a rescue, without even pausing to remove any of his clothing. Grabbing the sinking child by her hair, Kirkland and his wife, who had also come to help, managed to pull the girl from the pit - without the assistance of Mrs Kirkland, it was believed that it would have been a double tragedy, as so often happens when people attempt a rescue with no thought for their own safety.

Some months later, before a large assembly at the Council Room, Mr Kirkland was presented with the Royal Humane Society award and a reward of five guineas.

Miscellaneous Accidents

The roofs of two new houses which were nearing completion on School Lane in early 1865, collapsed with disastrous consequences for a neighbouring property. Most of the roof and supporting brickwork fell into the adjoining locksmith's workshop, owned by Edward Haynes, which was in use at the time.

All of those employed in the workshop escaped without injury except for an elderly man, William Roberts, who was almost buried under the rubble. Mr Roberts suffered head and other injuries although he seems to have recovered despite his age. The accident was thought to be due to a combination of factors; the supporting timbers were of insufficient size and there was also a substantial weight of snow upon the roof.

Mr Haynes' lock-making workshop was most likely one of the few remaining in the area. Lock-making had been strong in Coven and Brewood for decades, run on a co-operative basis from numerous small village workshops. With the rise of mass-production, such work had all but gone to Willenhall and Wolverhampton by the time of this event. The snappily titled "Wolverhampton and Brewood Industrial and Provident Plate-Lock Manufacturing Society Ltd" was finally wound up in 1879.

When seven-year-old Thomas Evans went to the Harvest Supper hosted at Somerford Hall on Saturday 15th July 1848, his parents could never have expected it to be the cause of his death. While at the event he drank a quantity of ale, then set off for home at about 10pm with another boy. Thomas was sick several times en route and had to be carried part of the way. At home he lay in a stupor until around 2am, when he suffered the first of several fits. The convulsions continued throughout the day and he finally passed away at about three in the afternoon.

At the inquest, held at the Admiral Rodney, surgeon James McMunn said that Thomas was a very delicate boy and that less than two pints of strong ale could easily have brought on the convulsive fits which led to his death. The jury decided that he died as a result of "the innocent administration of an intoxicating beverage", no doubt to the great relief of those who were in charge of serving food and drink at the meal.

The boy's father was John Evans, and a man of that name who was a labourer at Brewood at the time was brought before Penkridge Petty Sessions for failing to comply with an order to maintain his mother. Whether it was the same man is not clear but the offender in this case was jailed for 3 months, being unable to pay the fine imposed due to his distressed circumstances.

William Bradfield decided to chase after a rabbit while he was harvesting at Brewood in August 1869. During the pursuit he fell over his own scythe, badly lacerating his leg. He was conveyed to the hospital in Wolverhampton where his condition was reported as very low due to loss of blood.

In June 1890 a seventeen-year-old lad by the name of Johnson died following a horrendous accident. He somehow fell into a boiler full of hot water at Blackladies Farm, where he was employed by William Pedley, and was severely scalded. He was initially attended to by Dr Garman and later conveyed to Wolverhampton Hospital but he died some hours later.

Guns and Poaching

A fatal firearms accident occurred at Engleton in early 1842. Farmer Mr Smith Muchall had gone off to bed at about 10:30pm when he was alarmed by the barking of his dogs. Having suffered several break-ins in the recent past, he kept his loaded gun in his bedroom. Looking from his window he saw a man walking about the property, and taking aim, delivered a fatal shot. Unfortunately the victim was his groom, Samuel Jervis who seems to have gone out to see why the dogs were barking. It seems that no charge was brought against Mr Muchall; both men were in their early 20s.

Twenty-eight-year-old John Onions and a man named Mullingar were unloading a cart of bran at The Hattons in 1885, when the latter came across a gun lying in the cart. Not realising that it was loaded he picked it up, and while turning it in his hands it went off, the charge entering Mr Onions and killing him outright. The inquest held at Brewood returned a verdict of 'accidental death' but Mullingar was severely censured for his behaviour.

William Wootton, a local labourer, was fined over £1 including costs for having a gun without a license in March 1886. Constable Hurmson told the Petty Sessions at Penkridge that he heard a gun fired at Hill Top at about half past seven in the evening and went to investigate. He found Wootton and his friend in the vicinity but neither appeared to have a weapon. Suspecting that they had concealed the gun, a search revealed that they had broken it down, with Wootton having the barrel and the other man, Evans, hiding the stock and a catapult. Twenty-three-year-old Wootton, whose father was a shoemaker on Dean Street, admitted ownership and the fact that he didn't have a license.

Taking animals that belong to someone else, or taking wild animals from someone else's land, has gone on since time out of mind. Although no less a crime than any other form of theft, it is easy to sympathise with the unemployed labourer who might have taken the odd pheasant or rabbit to feed his starving family. For others though, poaching was simply a way of making money and they frequently went armed, with no compunction about using their weapons against whoever should try to stop them.

Constable Holloway caught two poachers by chance near the Bell Inn. As he passed Charles Colley and Andrew Thomas he noticed that they each had something in their pockets. Nothing was forthcoming in answer to his enquiry so he decided to search them and found Colley to be carrying a gun and Thomas a dead, and still warm, rabbit. Both men were fined when the case was heard at Cannock in early 1866 although Colley's fine was three times that of the other man as he had been convicted of taking game on two previous occasions.

In 1865, two men were fined for trespassing on John Fox's land at Hockerhill Farm in search of game, and a man from the Penn Road, Wolverhampton, was fined for taking a hare on Mr Tollfree's land at Gunston.

Thirty-four-year-old George Craik, a shepherd who lived at Pearse Hay, appeared before Penkridge Petty Sessions in 1888 on a charge of poaching. George Rowley, a local gamekeeper, found a snare with a rabbit in it and watched the area for several hours to see if anyone returned for it. At 6am, Mr Craik appeared and took it up along with several other traps containing rabbits. He was fined £1 including costs and bound over in the sum of £5 for six months.

Five youngsters were charged with stealing mushrooms from Albert Whitehouse's land in September 1899 - they were variously fined between one and seven shillings.

Brewood labourer James Yates was charged at Cannock Petty Sessions with libelling Benjamin Oakley, a gamekeeper employed on the Chillington estate. Yates had previously worked under Oakley as a night-watchman but had failed to follow instructions on numerous occasions and was eventually sacked. It seems that Yates wanted to get revenge on Oakley for being dismissed and he said in the presence of at least two people that he intended to get some handbills printed that would detail how Oakley was killing and selling game for his own personal benefit, something which was strictly forbidden for gamekeepers to do.

In due course several people received these printed bills which read:

> "B. Oakley, Chillington, game and rabbit destroyer, and his wife the seller of the same in county and town – T.Y".

In court, it was revealed that Yates had delivered the bills to numerous individuals and even nailed one to a tree in the Avenue on the approach to Chillington. At least one person said that Yates had boasted about having the leaflet printed and said that the printer had made a mistake with the initials but he was going to have them changed to "J.Y.". He also planned to put some leaflets in Mr Giffard's coach when he attended church.

Yates' lawyer cross-examined Mr Oakley as to whether or not he had killed rabbits and sent them to dealers for sale. Oakley said that he regularly killed rabbits as part of his job but categorically denied ever having sold one for personal gain. This was the essence of the defence case, that the allegation against Oakley was true, but the Magistrate said whether or not it was true, it was not a matter for public concern; Yates should have taken up the matter with Oakley's employer if he suspected misconduct. The prosecution offered to drop the charge if Yates would make an apology and cover expenses but he refused to do so and was committed to the Assizes for trial.

Escapes

Twenty-two-year-old Charles Willetts, a former blacksmith of Brewood, was 5ft 1in tall, had flaxen hair and light grey eyes.

We know this because his description was circulated in Australia where he was wanted after escaping from the prisoners' barracks. He had been tried at Stafford in 1822 and was transported on the convict ship 'Competitor'. He seems to have served about 4 years of his 7 year term.

In 1841, Constable George Newman took out an advertisement in the Staffordshire Advertiser to thank the Penkridge Association for the Prosecution of Felons for not taking any action against him; a prisoner in his custody, who had been charged with a felony against one of their members, had managed to escape.

Two men escaped from another, unnamed, Brewood Constable in 1845. In addition to the robbery they had committed at Brewood, William Brough and Joseph Wright were wanted for a number of offences in Wolverhampton. As they escaped they gave the officer a severe beating and stole his handcuffs. Police searching houses known to have been used by Brough discovered a large number of skeleton keys, which were said to be "thoroughly scientific instruments, and admirably adapted to pass any lock they may fit".

Twenty years later, another Brewood Constable was seriously assaulted while trying to make an arrest. The details presented at court were as follows. Two youths, Sydney Smith and Andrew Thomas, were creating a disturbance in Market Place between 11 and 12 pm and when Constable McCusker arrived at the scene he told them both to go home. Smith refused and as P.C. McCusker approached him, he punched the officer in the face and ran off. As the constable pursued him, Smith stopped and began throwing stones, one of which hit McCusker on the thigh. Following Smith further, Thomas suddenly reappeared with a number of other men, putting the officer in a dangerous position. McCusker had the sense to summon help and was soon joined by another constable and a young man.

The three made their way to the home of John Spilsbury, an acquaintance of Smith and listening at the door, hear Smith and Thomas talking about what they would do to Constable McCusker given the chance. Banging the door, McCusker demanded entrance to the house, saying that he wanted Smith, but it was Spilsbury who opened the door, brandishing a poker.

Spilsbury told the officer that if he tried to enter the house he would "split his ___ skull open" but McCusker nevertheless stepped inside. Spilsbury immediately struck the officer three very violent blows to the head and the attack only ended when the other constable managed to pull his colleague out of the house.

In summing up, Magistrate Mr Evans severely reprimanded Smith and advised him to change his ways before he got much older. He was fined 20 shillings plus costs or twenty one days with hard labour in default.

Sentencing 24 year-old Spilsbury, he said that although he had committed a brutal assault, he still appeared to have some redeeming qualities, not least that he had recently saved the life of another man. In view of this he was given a comparatively light £3 fine or a month with hard labour in default. The case against the other youth, Thomas, was dismissed as there was no evidence that he had used any violence.

Another Brewood policeman was beaten-up by two men in

1892. Constable Elliott had been called to eject the men from the Stirrups Inn, but en route to the police station, he was punched and kicked by his prisoners William and John Summerton. Cannock Magistrates handed John a £2 fine and William 21 days in prison.

Cornelius Boyle, a Scotsman, was locked up in the police cell one evening in September 1865. Constable Harrison checked on him at 3am and finding all to be in order returned to his bed but a little while later, he heard a knocking coming from the direction of the cell. Going down to investigate, he found that Boyle was trying to dig his way out of the cell! The prisoner had broken the lid off the toilet and thereby obtained a large nail, with which he had removed some bricks from the floor and dug out a quantity of sand and soil beneath. He was transferred to Penkridge, where the cells were presumably more secure.

A different type of escape was sought by John Greensmith, a wealthy farmer of Lapley Hall. He escaped life itself when he committed suicide in February 1873. Mr Greensmith, who was in his mid-40's, hung himself by means of a neckerchief tied to his bedpost. He left a wife and six children.

Frances Barber, a fifty-six-year-old woman hung herself at her brother's farm in Bishops Wood. Miss Barber had been in the Staffordshire Lunatic Asylum, but as her condition seemed to have improved, she was permitted to return to the farm where she was able to help her brother John with day-to-day tasks. In the last weeks of her life however her state of mind had become very variable. Finally, at 3am one August morning, when her brother came downstairs, he found her hanging from a beam in the kitchen, quite dead. The inquest jury returned a verdict of suicide while in a state of temporary insanity.

Finally, we have two people who escaped in search of a better life together. A woman leaving her husband for a widower is hardly likely to make the news these days, unless vulnerable children are perhaps involved. In 1886 however, it was considered quite scandalous and worthy of putting into print. It must have set tongues wagging in the village and further afield when Eliza Davies of Kiddemore Green, ran away with her 38-year-old neighbour, Edward Ward, who had been widowed a couple of years earlier.

The pair had made careful plans to elope; Ward, who was a wagoner in the employ of Mr Crane, had given a week's notice and arranged for a broker to buy all his possessions. When the dealer came to collect the goods he also conveyed the runaways' luggage to Wolverhampton. Ward arranged for his eldest daughter Sarah, aged 10, to be sent to relatives in Stafford but the couple took his youngest daughter, Susan aged 6, along with them. Mr Ward's son aged 17 was left to fend for himself, although he was out of work.

George Davies, who was also a wagoner, was left to look after a daughter of 11 and son of 13. To add insult to injury, his wife took most of his last fortnight's wages which had been paid to him the evening before she disappeared.

Chapter 3
Damage, Cruelty & Theft

Before delving into the details of specific crimes committed in Brewood, it is worth briefly considering how the law was applied in practice during the nineteenth century. There was no police force in the modern sense until the 1850s; before this there was an 'area constable', assisted by watchmen, acting under the supervision of a Justice of the Peace who was in turn appointed by the crown - a system that had been in place since medieval times. Landowners and farmers also availed themselves of gamekeepers and bailiffs to protect their interests. When public order was threatened, as it sometimes was by striking workers or those with a political or religious grievance, there was little option but to call out the army to protect the peace.

There were essentially three tiers of justice in the Victorian era; Petty Sessions, sometimes referred to as Police Courts, were the forerunners of Magistrates' Courts and dealt with lower level crimes, and later, licensing and other such matters. These were held at police stations or local chambers sometimes known as 'justice rooms'. Matters requiring a higher court were sometimes passed to the Quarter Sessions, so called because they were held quarterly, at Stafford. The most serious crimes, and occasionally civil matters, were referred to the Assizes and the 'circuit judges'.

Just as there were few qualms about putting children to work in laborious and dangerous positions in the first half of the nineteenth century, so there was little compunction in bringing youngsters before a formal court for comparatively minor offences - everyone had to abide by the rules, without exception.

Those charged with offences committed at Brewood were usually tried at Penkridge, Cannock or Wolverhampton Police Courts where the magistrate could hand down a fine or a custodial sentence, which might also include hard labour at the 'house of correction'. Hard labour would often consist of picking oakum; that is, unravelling the individual fibres from tarred ropes for re-use as caulking[1]. It was extremely hard and dirty work, usually resulting in severely blistered and blackened hands.

Hard labour at a prison might include being made to walk the treadmill. A few such man-powered mills created an end product, flour for example, but most produced nothing and were used solely as a form of punishment. An alternative to the treadmill was the crank, an equally pointless hand operated machine with variable resistance - both were despised by prisoners. Those sentenced to hard labour were also frequently put to the task of stone-breaking or used as labour for road and

---
1   A filling between planks used in boat-building

dock construction. The gravest offences might result in extended prison terms or ultimately in capital punishment. Transportation for a specified number of years or for life was often used for lesser crimes, rarely for the most serious or capital offences.

Damage

There are very few reported cases of wanton criminal damage in Brewood during the 1800s. A charge of arson brought against seventeen-year-old Edward Picken in October 1843 is a rarity in the locality, probably because the sentences involved for such offences were very severe. He was transported for fifteen years for setting fire to a haystack belonging to Henry Southwick of Harvington Birch.

Joshua Leek, a local cordwainer (shoemaker), and his friend Rogers, were fined fourpence each (plus costs of 10 shillings or more) for damage to a boat owned by Mr Giffard. The boat was tied up at Belvide Reservoir when the pair decided to take a Sunday row around the pool. Before long they were hailed by Thomas Price, Mr Giffard's agent, so they rowed back to shore and left the boat in his charge. No evidence was given as to the damage caused, it seems more likely to have been a token fine for 'taking without consent'.

Mary Hunt of Newport Street, and her children, Sarah and Henry, found themselves in court on the day before Christmas Eve 1857, charged with causing damage to Holly trees owned by T.W. Giffard of Chillington. Mrs Hunt said that a gentleman at Brewood required some Holly and because her husband William was presently out of work, she and the children went to collect some. The prosecution told the court that Mr Giffard did not wish to press the charge, merely to stop the practice - in this case by making an example of a poor woman and her children. The 3 shillings in expenses imposed by the Magistrate cannot have have added greatly to the Hunt family Christmas.

Cruelty

A man named Brew was sentenced to a month in prison in 1820 for baiting a bull in Market Place. Although the practice was not outlawed until some fifteen years later, he was was found guilty of creating a nuisance.

A shocking act of animal cruelty was perpetrated by Brewood 'coal jagger' Edward Ellmore. In 1835, Ellmore was selling coal from his cart at Four Crosses, on Watling Street, when his horse steadfastly refused to set off. Frustrated at being unable to get on with his work, he took a quantity of straw, placed it beneath the animal and set fire to it. As the poor creature still refused to move, he proceeded to whip it without mercy. The horse was so badly burned that it died the following day and a witness told the court at Wolverhampton that its skin was so lacerated that it was like jelly. According to the Wolverhampton Chronicle:

> *"The defendant, who affected to cry during the hearing of the case, said that he had been over-persuaded to do it by a person at Wolverhampton, and that he would not do it again for the world's worth".*

The case naturally evoked a sense of disgust in the courtroom and, after admonishing him for his inhuman conduct, the Magistrate imposed a fine of 20 shillings plus costs.

Henry Anslow was fined for continuously working his horse while it was in an unfit state, without regard for its well-being. An RSPCA Inspector visited Brewood after being told about the matter and, accompanied by Sergeant Whitehouse, called upon Mr Anslow. The animal was found to be very old and emaciated, lame in three legs with one leg having an inflamed hock. Confronted with an independent assessment of the animal's condition, Anslow said "I know it has been bad for some time, I intend to get the keeper to shoot it. I only drew a little coal with it.". By the time the matter came to court, Sergeant Whitehouse was able to confirm that the horse had indeed been destroyed. Nevertheless, Anslow was fined 2s 6d with almost twice that in costs.

Henry Holbeach, a market carrier of Hill Top, was found guilty of cruelty to a mare in his possession in 1901, presumably also for using it when in an unfit condition. In this case the fine was slightly reduced because he had at least tried to ease the animal's pain.

Theft & Robbery

As long as people have had possessions, so we have had theft. While some of the stolen items mentioned in the following stories might seem surprising, it is worth reminding ourselves of the obvious point that if someone could steal a thing, they would not have to pay for it. While theft was by no means perpetrated only by the poor, many people in this era had very little if any 'disposable income' and thousands lived in true poverty. As a result, what might today seem to be a trivial item of clothing, furniture, equipment or food, may have presented too tempting a target to someone in extreme deprivation.

While houses, farms, shops and public houses were obvious targets for thieves, canal wharves, with their boats and warehouses, were another source of 'rich pickings'. In addition to industrial resources such as coal and iron ore, the canals were used to transport a host of other materials and goods. Bulk materials included lime, manure and slate, but a range of more easily pilfered items such as timber, metal castings, furniture, household goods and groceries were also conveyed. These items, and especially coal, often fell prey to thieves, sometimes from among the boatmen or employees of the industries concerned.

The seriousness with which theft was treated can be seen from the case of thirty-eight-year-old Thomas Green, who was executed at Stafford Gaol on the first Saturday in September 1813. He had stolen a horse, a very valuable commodity, belonging to a Mr W Kendrick of Brewood. Green and two other men had the dubious honour of being the first to be hung on the newly constructed gallows in front of the prison.

The marvellously named John Jump, aged 47, was found not guilty of stealing a silver watch, and over four guineas belonging to John Davies at Brewood in 1817. A severe penalty would no doubt have been imposed had he been convicted. Thieves who stole two flitches (sides) of bacon from the house of William Westwood of The Pavement a decade later escaped without detection and also avoided a hefty sentence.

Contrast the hanging of Thomas Green with the much lighter punishment of Thomas Downes, who was tried at Stafford twenty years later on five separate counts of theft. He was alleged to have stolen a large number of tools from different individuals in Brewood. He was found guilty on three counts and sentenced to over 6 months imprisonment, with two weeks to be served in solitary confinement – a sentence immeasurably less harsh than that meted out to Green.

A charge of theft brought against William Shale of Brewood was easily proven and he was also given a six month sentence, the goods in this case being 10lbs of wheat stolen from a neighbouring farm. On a Saturday evening in the summer of 1829, Shale was chatting to John Evans, who was threshing wheat on Mr Careless' farm. When the farmer went to look at the wheat in his barn the next morning, he found the door difficult to open. Once he had managed to gain access, he saw that the grain was much disturbed and it looked as though some had been taken.

In due course, Mr Shale was arrested and charged with the theft. At court he didn't deny taking the wheat but told the jury that both he and Evans had agreed to take some because their wives were both very partial to 'frummetry', a pudding made from wheat boiled in milk and flavoured with sugar and cinnamon.

Joseph Bill of Hyde Mill told the court that Shale's daughter brought some wheat to him for grinding on the Saturday night. Shale's daughter Emma, who was about 8 years old, was then called to give evidence against her father! She told the court that he had brought home some wheat on the Saturday and sent her off to the miller to have it ground.

A sample of Mr Careless' remaining wheat was shown to the jury and John Evans said that it looked like his master's grain because it had traces of the weeds 'vetch' and 'drake' mixed in with it. He completely refuted Shale's assertion that the two men had each agreed to take some of the wheat. Needless to say, the jury found William Shale guilty and for trying to besmirch the reputation of Mr Evans, the judge decided that one week of the sentence should be spent in solitary confinement. Incidentally, John Mullard, a labourer of 'Court Lane' (a short road with half a dozen dwellings, which lay off Sandy Lane) was acquitted for stealing wheat in the previous year.

The following thefts reveal more examples of what people considered worth stealing and what the penalties were if they were caught.

Robert Breeze was sentenced to one month in prison plus hard labour for stealing potatoes belonging to John Phillips. In addition, the first and last three days of his term were to be served in solitary confinement.

In imitation of the rhyme featuring the piper's son, 46-year-old Thomas Blakemore stole a pig from John Aston at Brewood in 1834. This 'Tom', didn't go 'roaring down the street' after a beating however - he was transported for 7 years.

In 1838, Thomas Spicer was committed for trial for stealing a "neat's tongue and a chawl of bacon" from Brewood butcher Charles Day.

George Padeley and George Lewis were indicted for stealing 23 chickens from Mr Smith Muchall (senior) of Engleton in 1839. Assiduous detective work by the local police enabled them to follow the offenders' footprints all the way back to Cannock! At the conclusion of their trial at Stafford, the Chairman told the court that the pair had been convicted of several offences in the past and that "it would be trifling with justice to allow them to remain in this country any longer". Both were transported for seven years.

In 1841 there was a spate of thefts of chickens in the area - on one spring evening, no less than thirty birds were stolen from Mr Ingram's hen-house and a reward of £10 was offered for information leading to a conviction. In the same year, Joseph Wright was charged with stealing currants from John Adey's garden; the Wolverhampton court ordered that he pay a shilling to Mr Adey, the value of the stolen fruit, and a fine of 5 shillings plus costs. Not having the means to pay he was committed to prison for a month.

Three men, Griffiths, Bonner and Lines, were discovered hiding in a haystack near some cottages and charged with attempting to commit a robbery. The trio had been begging in the area during the day and when Constable Smalley moved them on they said they were going to Stafford that evening. The Wolverhampton court were told that one of the inhabitants of the cottages heard footsteps outside during the night and sprung a rattle*. Hearing this, neighbour Thomas Lloyd alerted officer Smalley and they discovered the three miscreants hiding nearby. As the cottages lay in the opposite direction to Stafford,

---

* The same device as a football rattle, it was used by watchmen and those in isolated locations as a form of alarm.

the court decided that it was their intention to commit a theft and the three men were each committed to the House of Correction for fourteen days.

One day in 1849, James Lewis drew up his cart on the Codsall Road, hopped over a fence and began to help himself to hay from a nearby rick. Robert Walker, one of Mr Giffard's employees, saw Lewis tossing the hay over the fence to his lad, who was busy loading it onto their cart. When apprehended by Walker, Lewis admitted the offence and begged to be forgiven, but Mr Giffard decided that the matter should be brought to court. At the Wolverhampton hearing, Mr Lewis again admitted the offence and said he was a fool for acting so rashly. He was offered bail but committed for trial, the outcome however is not known.

In 1848, three men were fined a shilling each plus costs of over 10 shillings for stealing produce from the garden of Sarah Wright. John Barlow, James Jones and Samuel Hicken would serve fourteen days if they were unable to pay the amount prescribed by Wolverhampton Police Court. Barlow was also charged with assaulting John Westwood of Sparrows End who tried to stop him as the three walked off after the robbery. For that offence he was fined a further shilling plus costs or an additional fourteen days in default.

Henry Lloyd, a labourer of Kiddemore Green, was apprehended by Joseph Edge after breaking in to workmen's cottages owned by Mr Wilson of Whiteladies. Lloyd had carefully removed a window pane at each cottage, allowing him to open the casement and thereby gain access. When collared, he was sat in one of the cottages enjoying a feast of bread, bacon and currant loaf. When the local constable arrived Lloyd also confessed to stealing a watch and revealed where he had hidden it. He was sent for trial at Stafford but the outcome is not known.

Samuel Challinor was sentenced to be transported for ten years by the judge at Stafford Assizes in 1851. It was the third time he had been convicted of a felony, in this instance stealing a counterpane from Edward Hailes of Long Birch farm.

In the following month, Thomas Cooke was also transported for 10 years for stealing 70lbs of bacon and other items from John Fernie, a Congregational Minister of Sandy Lane. One morning Mr Fernie's daughter-in-law found the back door of the house open, when it had been securely locked the night before. In due course it was found that two flitches of bacon, two hams, two chawls and some clothing had been stolen.

Nine days later, Constable Batkin was walking along the canal tow-path when he encountered Cooke carrying a large bag on his back. When questioned about its contents, 19 year-old Cooke said it was rags and bones but the officer was not convinced and decided to examine it. As soon as Cooke put the bag on the ground, he ran off in the direction of Wolverhampton and Batkin gave chase.

After running a considerable distance, Cooke was grabbed by a man name Turner and held until Batkin caught up. He was found to be wearing a shirt and neck-cloth belonging to Mr Fernie and later admitted that he and two others had carried out the robbery. He told the court at Stafford Quarter Sessions that he took part in the burglary because he was fearful of the other two men involved, neither of whom had been apprehended.

In 1854, collier William Jones was indicted for stealing a pair of boots at Brewood. The man was in the kitchen at Mary Jarvis' house where he had been meeting a lodger and when he left, a pair of boots which had been hanging on a nail had disappeared. Later in the day, Jones was in the tap room of the Angel Inn, where he sold the boots to the Wolverhampton postman. Landlord John Fox advanced the money to the postman but kept the boots as security. When he found out that they were stolen, he handed them over to constable Gardener.

Jones had several previous convictions for theft and this time he was given six months hard labour. By way of comparison, in the same year, Harriet Simkiss was sentenced to three months imprisonment plus hard labour for stealing four chickens from John Higgs.

In 1860, four men who came to the Brewood Wakes dropped in at the Admiral Rodney. While there, they admired the pigeons kept by the landlord, George Richards, and asked to buy them. Mr Richards refused to sell at the price they were offering and later discovered that the birds had been stolen. While the four were found guilty of the theft, the Quarter Sessions jury recommended leniency; Joseph Bentley and Samuel, John and Leonard Evans, were each sentenced to four months imprisonment with hard labour.

James Young was imprisoned for three months for stealing the coat of local maltster William Lees of 'The Bargate' in 1864 but Mr Lees fell victim to another, much more serious crime three years later, when he visited the Crown Inn on Watling Street (near the Bell Inn) on business. When he arrived, he found that the landlord was away and he was asked by a woman to go into the kitchen to try and quieten a group of Irishmen who were making a disturbance. Courageously entering the building, he was immediately set upon by the men, who knocked him to the floor and savagely kicked him. Mr Lees suffered injuries to his head and face, lost four teeth and was confined to bed for over a fortnight as a result of the vicious attack.

The men absconded immediately after the assault but one of them, Michael Brannon, must have had suffered some remorse as he subsequently gave himself up and entered a guilty plea when the case came to court. Brannon received an excellent character report from several respectable local inhabitants and this, when added to the fact that he had surrendered, meant that he was fined £2 rather than imprisoned for six weeks.

Thomas Beech, a Church Eaton butcher, became intoxicated while at one of the village public houses, and while in this condition, he was relieved of his purse containing £54 - a huge amount of money to carry about the person in 1865. Thomas Wilkes, a 30-year-old labourer who was in the pub at the same time, was later seen with a purse similar to the stolen one. When apprehended, he was found to be carrying a large sum of money and had also recently purchased a gun, both of which seemed beyond his means. Wilkes alleged that he had found one of the missing banknotes in the road and the rest of the money he had saved up by going without food in order to fund his plan to emigrate to America. The jury at the Quarter Sessions failed to be drawn in by his explanation and he was sentenced to six months with hard labour.

In 1850, James Francis Bate was found guilty of stealing two rabbit traps belonging to Joseph Beech of The Hattons. He was sentenced to be imprisoned for a month and to be whipped once.

In the following year, two men, William Highway and William Hammersley were found guilty of stealing a bag and nineteen chickens from Mr Beech. Highway, having a previous conviction for stealing a saddle and bridle, was transported for seven years and the other man was imprisoned for twelve months.

The thieves were caught in the act a little after midnight on 8th January. Constable Batkin was patrolling the canalside near the farm when he saw a number of individuals acting suspiciously. He immediately went to the farm and together with Mr Beech, kept an eye on the premises. They soon noticed a light in the boiler-house and then another in the adjoining hen roost. After much disturbance amongst the hens, a figure emerged at the doorway and after looking about, called to someone else to "bring the bag". Beech and Batkin took the opportunity to swoop as the men were dragging the fully-laden bag out of the boiler-house. It contained sixteen birds and there were a further three in the roost, all with their necks wrung.

In their defense at the Stafford Quarter Sessions, the pair denied attempting to steal the birds and claimed they were merely there to sleep in the hen-house!

Robert Robinson of Wolverhampton was employed as a horse-breaker by Mr Beech in the mid 1860s. During the six weeks or so that the man had worked there, the farm had lost a substantial number of fowl. One day, another farm worker, John Travers, found two dead birds amongst some straw in the stables. He told his master, who duly informed the police, and that afternoon Constable Harrison arranged to intercept Robinson on his return to Wolverhampton.

Upon searching Robinson's trap the constable found three birds, six eggs, some leather straps and miscellaneous other items belonging to Mr Beech, and a search of his home turned up another two chickens. At Penkridge Police Court the defendant made a long rambling statement about why he had taken the leather straps and other items but could not convince the Bench of his innocence; he was sentenced to six months.

Labourer's daughter Harriet Cotterell was charged with stealing money from Joseph Fox (mentioned in a later chapter), a saddler who lived on Dean Street. On 21st February 1888, Mr Fox went out into his garden but when he returned to the house he found that 4 shillings was missing from a drawer. He found fourteen-year-old Harriet begging nearby, followed her down the street and accused her of taking the money, at which point she ran away. Mr Fox chased after her but when he caught up with her she turned about and said "Now search me!". Fox held onto the girl until a policeman arrived and as the three walked back toward the police station, Fox and the officer each picked up coins that the girl had tried to dispose of. Enoch Plant, who was in the street at the time the money was taken, said he saw Cotterell walking down Fox's entry with the money in her hand. The Bench at Penkridge Police Court imposed a fine and costs of £2.

A 12-year-old Brewood girl named Rosannah Holland was

imprisoned for 10 days for stealing a letter from William Storer, an assistant overseer of the poor, who lived at Shutt Green. Mr Storer had left the letter containing two cheques, to the value of £327, lying on his lawn when Miss Holland, who was selling pegs, called at his house. After she had left the letter was nowhere to be found. The Cannock Magistrate decided that the girl would be better off away from her family and in addition to the sentence, had her sent to a reformatory school for 4 years.

In 1888, a thirteen-year-old lad named Patrick Tighe was charged with stealing two bags of bones from brothers Edward Whitehouse (mentioned elsewhere), butcher and landlord of the Bridge Inn, and Albert, also a butcher. Constable Lawton told the court that he arrested the boy at the Reading Room and the lad admitted taking both bags. In his defence, the boy said he had taken the first bag to sell so he would not go home without money for his widowed mother, and the second to pay for his 4d monthly subscription to the Reading Room. The lad was found guilty and sentenced to twelve strokes of the birch. We might pity Patrick Tighe for being given corporal punishment while apparently trying to look after his mother and better himself. However, neither he nor his mother may have been quite the innocent characters as they might at first seem.

Mrs Tighe had been a widow since Patrick was a small child. In 1881, she was a lodging-house keeper living on Sandy Lane but three years later, her situation must have taken a turn for the worse as she was fined for being drunk in Market Place. By 1891, Mrs Tighe, her two sons and mother-in-law all lived in rooms at the Bridge Inn, supported by 'Parish Pay & Children's Help'.

Following on from the case against young Tighe, Thomas and Eliza Moore, described as 'marine store dealers' (probably running a general store catering to canal users) were charged with receiving the stolen goods. Patrick Tighe had already told the court that he had sold the bones to the Moores, and both bags had been found on the premises, although the couple denied knowing that the bones were stolen. The Bench decided that as they had paid less than they were worth, and that they must have known the position of Tighe's mother, they knew full well that they were receiving stolen goods. They were fined 20 shillings plus costs. Three years after this case, Thomas Moore and his family were living at Bargate Cottages; his occupation was then described as a 'hawker', that is, an itinerant trader of goods.

When Patrick Tighe was nineteen he was once more in court, this time on a charge of burglary from the farmhouse of Mr Blewitt at Somerford. The case initially came before Cannock Petty Sessions but Tighe was committed for trial at Stafford. The farmer's son, Ernest, testified that Patrick Tighe had been employed by his father up until a few months earlier to sell milk, but had since left. On the day before the burglary, Tighe had attended an auction at the farm and had hung around afterwards, driving horses and cattle about. Ernest Blewitt told him he had no right to be there and ordered him off the land.

At about 1am Mr Blewitt found several doors of the property to be open so he locked them up. Later he found that a brown coat which had been hanging in the hall was missing, a ham had disappeared from their larder and two panes of glass in the laundry were broken. In the morning a domestic servant noticed that the stable door was open and inside she saw Tighe, fast asleep. Another farm servant, Thomas Warner, woke Tighe and asked him whether he planned to remain there all day, at which point he got up.

By coincidence, Edward Whitehouse now came to the property to borrow one of Mr Blewitt's ponies, and he saw Tighe in the yard wearing a brown coat. After putting the pony in the trap, Tighe came up to him and said "I have got part of a ham here. If I put it in a bag will you put it in the trap and take it to Brewood for me? If any of the men say anything to you, say it is a feed of corn for the pony". Mr Whitehouse, no doubt with earlier events in mind, refused to get involved.

Tighe later came to the house and handed the coat to a servant saying "this is not my coat", but when asked what he was doing with it, he said someone had given it to him. Mrs Blewitt instructed Warner to search the stable after Tighe had left and the missing ham was found in the loft. The matter was reported to the police and Constable Beresford was detailed to keep watch on the area to see if anyone returned for the stolen ham, but they did not.

Sergeant Whitehurst and Constable Beresford arrested Tighe at his home the following Sunday. When charged he admitted wearing the coat, which he now said he had found in the stable, but denied breaking-in to the house and stealing the ham. The jury at Stafford decided that there was insufficient evidence to prosecute and Patrick Tighe was acquitted.

Now, Mr Whitehouse himself was no stranger to the police. In 1884 he had brought a charge of assault against Arthur Spendlove, a former Brewood policeman, to which the constable served a cross-summons alleging the same offence. The men had been on the platform at Four Ashes station, Whitehouse waiting for his father to return from a greyhound coursing event and Spendlove waiting to travel to Rugeley, where he was now stationed, after conducting some business in Brewood.

Whitehouse claimed that after his father arrived and they were walking the dog along the platform, someone fell against him and then fell onto the track. According to his testimony, this person was Spendlove, who then climbed back onto the platform and accused Whitehouse of having his hat. When Whitehouse denied it, he said the other man struck him with a cane.

Spendlove's version of events was quite different. He told Penkridge Petty Sessions that as he was boarding the train, he was struck by Whitehouse, who also knocked his hat off. He was then struck a second time and fell onto the rails as a result. He said that Whitehouse used abusive language and put up his fists in a fighting stance. Spendlove told the court that he had reported Whitehouse's brother, Albert, for several offences in the past and he believed that this was the motive for Whitehouse to attack him. Witnesses were called for both sides but there being no clear evidence as to which party was telling the truth, the case was dismissed.

In 1884, Albert Whitehouse was summoned for having a dangerous dog but to show how placid the animal was, he produced it in court. The Fox Terrier pup was said to have bitten the two children of a gardener from Horsebrook, but Whitehouse told the court that the children had been teasing the dog and it had not actually bitten them. He was ordered to meet court costs and keep the dog under proper control in future. The children's father who brought the case was Alfred Yapp!

In 1899 Whitehouse was charged with "furious driving" along Congreve Lane but the case was dismissed. Finally, in 1914, he was summoned by a single woman, Ethel Bradshaw of Sparrows End, for failing to support their illegitimate child. Miss Bradshaw told Penkridge Police Court that he had since agreed to pay 3 shillings per week but the Bench decided it should be set at 3s 6d.

William Stoker was sentenced to 21 days with hard labour for stealing 7s 9d from his sister Louisa. She had left her purse in the pocket of a coat hanging on her bedroom door at their Newport Street home, but it wasn't there when she went to get it. As her brother was the only other person in the house at the time, he must have committed the theft. Although he initially denied it, he was later found to have spent some of the money at the Anchor Inn, Coven. This was not Stoker's only misdemeanour; at the same hearing, at Cannock Petty Sessions in 1892, he was given an additional seven days for a charge of 'being on premises at Brewood for an unlawful purpose', although no further detail is given.

Edgar Smith, a boatman, was sentenced to two months with hard labour for stealing a fork and shovel from a dung-heap beside the canal in 1893.

Henry Wenlock received a month with hard labour for stealing a pigeon from David Clarke in 1899. A neighbour saw him blithely walk into Clarke's yard, pick up a pigeon and take it off to his father's house.

Two men employed by the previously mentioned butcher Albert Whitehouse, ended up in court charged with stealing meat and a pair of braces! They slipped away early in the morning from Mr Whitehouse's Stafford Street premises, taking with them the aforementioned items. The two men, one employed as a cowman, the other as a wagoner, were arrested at Tettenhall some time later and brought before Cannock Petty Sessions. William Evans was jailed for a month and his accomplice Jones for two weeks, both with hard labour.

William Wakelam and his wife Hannah conducted a carriers business from their Newport Street home around the middle of the century. On a Monday in March 1862, Mrs Wakelam visited Wolverhampton market and purchased 14 shillings worth of lard. The container was fastened near the tail-board of her cart but when she got as far as Coven on the return journey she found that the vessel had disappeared. She informed the police who subsequently arrested two men, Edward Chambers and Henry Edwards, who were caught in possession of the lard while trying to sell it on.

At the Lent Assizes, the two men claimed that they had found the container of lard in the road and had carried it a long way to try to dispose of it. Mrs Wakelam said she did not believe that the container could have fallen from the vehicle and the court seemed to agree - the pair were each handed a sentence of four months imprisonment.

William Hand worked for Mr Wilson of The Hattons as a wagoner and returning to the farm one evening in 1841, he claimed that he had been accosted by three men near Pendeford. He told his employer that the men had thrown him to the ground and stolen his watch, 3 shillings and sixpence, his jacket and his cap. Mr Wilson immediately arranged for handbills to be issued to help track down the assailants and offered a fifty shilling reward for their capture. The two men went to Wolverhampton to inform the police, who arranged to visit all the local pawnbrokers in the hope of catching the offenders.

What no-one else knew was that Hand had completely invented the story, perhaps hoping that his employer would take pity on him and reward him financially for the supposed loss. Hand now realised that he was in over his head and, as he still had the watch in his possession, he decided to dispose of it. His attempt to do this was as harebrained as his original scheme because he took the watch to a pawnbroker in the town! The police were shortly informed and after obtaining a description of the man pawning the item they were able to identify Hand. No first-hand reason for the deception was given and whether or not any action was taken against Hand is unknown but it would seem highly likely that he at least lost his job.

A newspaper report of 1830 tells how a hawker of goods lost a substantial amount of money at the Red Lion (as it was then called). It was mid winter when he and several others were sitting in the kitchen drinking. At some point during the evening one of those present asked to see the man's license; he took out his pocket book containing the document and his money and showed the former to the interested party, after which he put it away in an inside pocket of his waistcoat.
When the man retired to bed, he found that he had somehow

been relieved of his entire purse which held the license, fourteen and a half sovereigns, and a £5 bill. Despite spending the whole of the next day searching for the culprit, he was unable to recover his loss. It seems that the pickpocket had a morsel of conscience however, as the pocket book, containing everything except the sovereigns, was pushed under the front door of the pub on the following night.

Finally, what seems to be the only reported case of highway robbery at Brewood, took place in 1831. The perpetrator, 23-year-old William Fenton was executed for taking a silver watch and several bank-notes from Matthias Southwick of Poole Hall, Trescott, near Lower Penn.

Chapter 4
Crimes Against The Person

An interesting local case was noted in the Staffordshire Advertiser back in 1822; a man was fined fifteen shillings for "fighting and for assaulting the constable in the execution of his duty in suppressing a tumult"! The fine itself is interesting because it was ordered to be paid in kind, in the form of bread distributed to the poor of the area. No detail is given about what constituted the commotion involved.

What must be one of the most innocuous 'assaults' ever recorded was brought before the Wolverhampton court in 1836. Two Brewood men, Thomas Foster and John Hill met at the Royal Oak on Watling Street (opposite the Bell Inn) and greeting the other man as "Jack", Mr Foster asked to shake hands. When Mr Hill refused, the other man took him by the arm and shook his hand anyway. Hill proceeded to press a charge of assault. Unsurprisingly, the Magistrate dismissed the case, although he did impose costs on the defendant. We can only guess that there was some sort of 'history' between the two men.

A charge of manslaughter levelled at a Brewood resident in 1857 excited a huge amount of interest locally and further afield. The case was all the more fascinating because it concerned ta man who was cut out of his wealthy father's will for marrying a woman below his station, the same woman he was now accused of killing.

Arthur Edwin Beaufoy Durant was the son of George Durant of Tong Castle. Elizabeth Harley, the daughter of an Albrighton tradesman, was employed as a live-in nursemaid at the castle. A relationship developed between Elizabeth and 'Beaufoy' and before long he announced his intention to wed his new found love. His father made clear his utter opposition to the idea and warned his son that he would be disinherited if he went ahead with the marriage. At this point, Beaufoy seemed to care much more for his bride-to-be than his inheritance and the couple were married at Birmingham on 14th December 1842 and settled down at Stone House, Boningale

Durant had been a Lieutenant in the army and had worked for the East India Company in Madras. There was clearly something peculiar about his character, one newspaper report saying that he was a person of very gentlemanly demeanour:

> *"but is evidently strongly imbued with that spirit of eccentricity for which his family are so remarkable".*

In 1854 Beaufoy Durant was declared bankrupt, although he

was still on half-pay from the Army, and the family moved from Boningale to Shutt Green. On 26th February 1857, forty-two-year-old Mrs Durant passed away. Following rumours of ill-treatment by her husband, her brother Edmund, a painter who lived at Pattingham, made a formal request to the Coroner for an enquiry.

The inquest began on a Monday at the Angel Hotel, at that time kept by John Fox. It was adjourned twice and was finally concluded on Saturday night of the same week. The jury, composed of notable individuals from the locality, heard evidence in front of a packed house and huge numbers of people thronged the streets outside. Beaufoy Durant, accompanied by his solicitor, was present throughout the proceedings.

Edmund Harley said that he had visited his sister a week or so before she died. She was lying in bed and at times was quite insensible. He didn't know what was wrong with her but he did notice that one of her eyes was bruised.

A Mrs Evitt of Harborne, who had known Elizabeth Durant for some months, visited her around the same time. She told the inquest that Mrs Durant was drifting in an out of sleep, although she seemed quite lucid while awake. She complained of a pain in her side but did not allege any ill-treatment. Two of Elizabeth's sisters were also present on that occasion and they pointed out the bruise on Elizabeth's eye and others on her legs and a particularly swollen bruise on her arm.

Harriet Harley was called to her sister on the day before she died. Elizabeth declared "Oh Harriet, I am dying!" and was complaining of pains in her side and her legs, both of which Harriet found to be very black and bruised. Surgeon Thomas Crean was also in attendance but no-one heard Mrs Durant say how she had received the injuries. Mrs Ann Smith was called as a witness at the request of Mr Durant. She stated that she had known the deceased for over a year, during which time she had been in ill-health and seemed to have a poor diet.

Mr Crean told the inquest that when he attended Mrs Durant she was complaining of pains in her head and he noticed she had a black eye. She was extremely emaciated and was at times delirious. The inquest was adjourned and the post mortem was conducted on the following day by Mr Crean and Dr Bidwell of Albrighton. When recalled, the surgeon said he had noted that the deceased had a black eye and a badly bruised and swollen arm. He found the body to be extremely emaciated and the stomach to be shrunken to the smallest size he had ever seen. Fluid around the brain seemed to be the cause of death but he could not say if it was the result of ill-treatment.

Apart from the bruising, it might be thought that Mrs Durant died as a result of some wasting disease or undiagnosed condition. However, two other witnesses gave evidence which supported the rumours that Mr Durant was a violent individual and he had caused the death of his wife. The first was Mary Ann Harley, who had lived with the couple for twelve years. She said that her sister's health began to fail about two years before she died. She recounted an episode from the previous Christmas when Mr and Mrs Durant had been out to supper. When they returned, Beaufoy Durant was drunk and very angry. Fearing for her safety, Mrs Durant left the house and spent several hours in a pigsty before returning. She also told the inquest how her sister had received the black eye; she said the couple were arguing and Mrs Durant called him a "blackguard wretch" at which Mr Durant threw a slipper that struck her in the eye. According to Miss Harley, Durant had ill-treated his wife for several years and she had eaten very little over the last 12 months.

The second witness was Ann Bird, the wife of shoemaker John Bird, who lived nearby. She added more detail to Mary Ann Harley's account of what had happened at Christmas, saying that the couple called in on her on their way home and left after a few minutes. Half an hour later Mrs Durant returned alone, not even wearing a shawl despite the freezing cold snow. She asked if she could come inside as she was in danger of her life from her violent husband who had been abusing her. She was about to enter Mrs Bird's house when she noticed two young men inside. She immediately drew back fearing that if her husband did come along, he would surely kill her if he found her in such circumstances. Instead, she crept off to the pigsty, where she spent three and a half hours before her sister came and took her home. Mrs Bird said that Mrs Durant had been to her house six or seven times over the winter before she died, seeking protection from her violent husband.

Mary Ann Harley was recalled in a state of great agitation. She told the jury that her sister had been forced to leave the family home on numerous occasions during the last winter and she had often found her huddling under hedges to avoid her husband.

The jury deliberated for some six hours, finally reaching a verdict of manslaughter at around 10pm. When the Coroner made out a warrant for committal, there was a scuffle between Durant and the three police officers who attempted to arrest him. Despite the evidence against him, it was said that the crowd seemed to be in favour of Mr Durant.

When the matter came before Stafford Assizes there was a brief review of the evidence but there being insufficient evidence to support the charge of manslaughter, Beaufoy Durant was found not guilty and he was discharged.

George Durant died in 1844 and stuck to his word with regard to his will. It seems quite possible therefore, that Beaufoy Durant came to blame his wife for his subsequent insolvency and the decline in his living standards. He and his two sons (the younger having the forenames 'Prince Albert') lived on Watling Street near Gailey railway station until his death in 1876. He continued to refer to himself as a 'gentleman' and 'retired officer'.

Thomas Weaver, a sixty-year-old bailiff living at Hattons Farm House, was fined one shilling plus costs at Wolverhampton Police Court in 1859, after being found guilty of striking a boy with his whip. The lad, Francis Rogers, claimed that he saw two children in the road who were about to be run over by Mr Weaver and he went to rescue them. He said that as Mr Weaver drew up, he struck him several times on his bare back with a whip causing a number of cuts. Weaver claimed that Rogers and the other children were playing marbles in the road and called upon them to move out of the way. He did not deny that he struck the child with his whip but claimed that he did so only once.

John Marshall, a young man said to have good connections and be holding a good situation, was fined £3, or six weeks with hard labour in default, for indecently assaulting an eleven-year-old girl in the village. His standing meant that he was able to pay the fine.

Joseph Lomas farmed at Brewood during the 1860s but he and his family lived an unhappy existence, with frequent verbal and physical assaults upon each other. In 1863, Mrs Lomas brought a charge of assault against her husband which was heard at Penkridge. The court were told that on April 1st, while in their kitchen, she had asked her husband if he could 'live peaceably' with her but received an offensive answer. When she retorted in a similar manner, he allegedly punched her and struck her with a poker. Mrs Lomas' daughter corroborated her mother's version of events but two male servants were called by Mr Lomas in his defence, both of whom said that his wife had started the row by calling her husband "a rogue and a vagabond". They claimed that she tried to kick him and that he had taken up the poker to defend himself against his son, who was siding with Mrs Lomas. The Bench believed Mrs Lomas' story and her husband was fined 1 shilling.

Francis Lomas, the 20-year-old son referred to, was a large and powerful man. On the Friday before the case, he had been apprehended on a warrant for threatening to do his father bodily harm. Not having the £25 surety to keep the peace towards his father, he had been committed to Stafford jail. When Joseph Lomas appeared in court, his arm and shoulder were said to be one mass of contusions as a result of an attack by his son. When Mr Lomas returned from Penkridge after pressing a charge against his son for the attack, he found his daughter had taken furniture and linen from his house. He intended to bring a charge of theft against her but withdrew it when advised that there appeared to be no felonious intent. It is not known what finally became of the family, except that by 1871 Francis Lomas had moved to Leek, where he was living alone as a farmer.

In 1864, William Hickin was fined 5 shillings for violently assaulting his wife, although it could easily have been Mrs Hickin who was in the dock. Mrs Hickin was correcting one of her children when her husband interjected and, after some words passed between them, he grabbed her by the hair and dragged her about the house. Mrs Hicken managed to grab the kitchen poker to try to beat him off but he wrested it from her and hit her three times across the back, before running off and locking himself in his workshop. The enraged woman proceeded to throw house-bricks and stones at him through the workshop window, but getting too close on one occasion, he struck her across the temple with the poker and she fell to the ground stunned. With typical tongue-in-cheek style, the Staffordshire Advertiser headlined their short report of the trial 'A Loving Couple'.

Thomas Spencer farmed at Bishops Wood in the 1870s but he was also an 'iron-master' - an owner of an iron-making business. Like so many wealthy people then and now, his over-inflated ego made him believe that he was above the law or, if he was guilty of a transgression, he could simply buy his way out of it. Unfortunately, class divisions in society often meant that he and others were right, at least as regards the latter.

In June 1871, he appeared before Wolverhampton Police Court

charged with assaulting Charles Chapman, a grocer, at Wolverhampton. Mr Chapman was driving his dog-cart along Berry Street in the town when he heard a voice behind cry out "Get out of the road!". Even if he had wanted to, he would have been unable to pull over, as there was an obstacle at the side of the road. Seconds later, the wheel of another cart locked with his but after a short distance, the wheels separated and the other vehicle began to overtake. Looking to the side to see who it was, Mr Chapman received a stinging blow across the face from the other man's whip. He followed the other vehicle as far as the entrance to the LNWR railway station where he found Spencer and his son alighting from the carriage, the elder man brandishing his whip as if to strike out again. Chapman remaining in his cart asked for the name and address of the other man to which he was told "I am well-known; my name is Spencer". As he was saying this, he struck the other man twice more with the whip, but Chapman was finally able to grab it to prevent further blows. A cabman named Nuttall, who was waiting outside the station, came up to help and as Chapman turned to see who it was, Spencer struck him on the back of the head.

A number of witnesses were called, all of whom agreed with Chapman's version of events with regard to the clash of vehicles and the subsequent assault. Spencer conducted his own defence, repeatedly questioning Chapman about the rules of the road, completely ignoring the true subject of the case. Nuttall told the court that Spencer had tried to bribe him to give false evidence. He said that Spencer came up to him after the assault and asked "Did you see him strike me on the side of the head?" to which he replied "No". Spencer then said "Will you be a witness for me, I will pay you your day's wages and something extra?" to which Mr Nuttall said nothing.

There was no doubt about the assault, but the Magistrate, as sometimes happened when there was an unevenness of wealth between parties, suggested that a settlement be made. Within a short while the solicitors had reached agreement, a sum of £20 being agreed upon, no doubt a sizeable sum to Mr Chapman. The Magistrate was spared from having to make a decision and Spencer escaped with his reputation intact, the whole affair having cost him nothing but an inconsequential sum of money.

Another case involving compensation rather than a decision took place a few years later. William Taylor junior, a local farmer, was examined at Penkridge Police court after allegedly assaulting labourer Thomas Hunt at the Brewood Wake in 1880. Taylor had asked the other man for liquor but when Hunt declined to give him any, Taylor was said to have dragged him off into a field and brutally bludgeoned him around the head. The court decided that the seriousness of the allegation meant that it should be passed to a higher authority and Taylor was committed for trial at Stafford.

During the case, heard at the Assizes just a few weeks later, the Assistant Chairman suggested that Taylor change his plea to guilty, pay £5 towards the court costs and £10 in compensation to Hunt, rather than face an inevitable custodial sentence if the jury were to find him guilty. Exactly why Taylor was offered this 'get out' was not reported; presumably it was because it was one man's word against another and there was doubt about who exactly had inflicted the injuries to Hunt.

Benjamin Brittle and his friend were sentenced to two weeks in prison for being drunk and disorderly in Brewood on Sunday 10th October 1886. After serving his sentence, Brittle, an iron-puddler from Wolverhampton, was brought before Cannock Petty Sessions to face a second charge: that he assaulted Mary Ann Sergeant, daughter of landlord at the Swan Inn. On the day in question, the men had entered the Swan but as they were already drunk, Mary ordered them off the premises. When she and her father tried to eject them, Brittle lashed out, hitting Miss Sergeant on her side. For the assault he was given a further three weeks, this time with hard labour.

Emma Wenlock brought a sexual assault charge against Henry Onions in the summer of 1849. She alleged that the assault happened twice, at two different places, at about 6pm in a lane near some cottages in Brewood. She told Wolverhampton Police Court that she had resisted the man's advances but didn't call out until she saw another man coming along the lane. Under cross examination, she admitted that she had had 'improper intercourse' with other men on previous occasions. The case was dismissed. According to the newspaper report Miss Wenlock was 17 years old, although an earlier census suggests she was two years younger.

It is all too easy to form a rose-tinted stereotypical view of people in the past - we might read the name of Mr Jones, the village baker, and instantly conjure up an image of a hearty fellow going about his daily business, dealing with customers and tending his ovens. It is a trap all too easy to fall into, forgetting that Mr Jones probably had good and bad sides to his character like any other person before or since. With this in mind, let us turn to Enoch Plant, a chimney-sweep who lived on Dean Street. Rather than the black-faced but happy-go-lucky character we might have been conditioned to envisage, this man and his son seem to have been most unpleasant characters.

On 17th November 1877, John Lilley a locksmith in his late 50s who lived at 2, Engleton Lane went to the Boat Inn. He took his beer into the 'parlour' where he saw Alfred Plant, Enoch's 25-year-old son, dancing. The younger man made some obscene remark to which Mr Lilley replied, at which point Plant tried to attack him. The quick-witted Mr Lilley threw his beer glass at Plant in order to stave off the attack and it caught him a glancing blow on the check. Enraged, Plant set about the older man, knocking him over a chair and continuing to beat him while he was on the floor. At this point the landlord intervened, stopped the assault and sent Lilley off home.

On his way back home, Lilley was accosted by Enoch Plant, who grabbed him and blew twice on a whistle to attract his son. When Alfred Plant arrived he asked "Father, have you got him?", to which his father replied "Yes, I have, now Alfred, kill the ___". Alfred Plant hit Lilley violently over the head with a 'knobble-stick', knocking him to the ground, and then proceeded to pummel him in the face with his fists. In his rage the young man cried out "I will murder you, you ___. I will make you remember". Mr Lilley's son George, who was nearby, witnessed the event but was powerless to intervene.

John Lilley suffered a badly fractured skull and serious concussion following the attack, and for a while was thought to be so close to death that his dying depositions were taken. Fortunately for Enoch Plant and his son, Mr Lilley recovered - they were each sentenced to 4 months imprisonment with hard labour for felonious wounding but they could so easily have been facing a charge of murder.

Just two years later Enoch Plant was back in court, this time at Birmingham, where he was found guilty of allowing a boy of 13 to climb a chimney. On this occasion he was fined £5 plus costs. An Act preventing the use of child chimney sweeps had been in force for forty years but some, like Plant, were prepared to blatantly flout it. The occupation had resulted in many children losing their lives through suffocation or burning. Furthermore, a particular form of cancer caused by breathing soot, was the first such disease that could be directly attributed to the workplace. Five years before Plant was prosecuted, another Bill had passed through Parliament, requiring that all sweeps be registered with the police in the area where they operated, thereby helping to enforce the applicable laws, so Plant could not even claim ignorance of the law.

Finally, in 1884, Enoch Plant found himself in court once again, this time at Penkridge on a charge of being drunk in Dean Street. He was fined 13 shillings including costs.

Two chimney sweeps, Thomas Malbon (23) and James Emery (18), were convicted of theft at Brewood in 1833. The pair crept into the stable loft of the Malt Shovel where an old ragman, William Weaver, was sleeping. They took his hat, shoes, socks and nightcap and all he got in return was a dusting of soot! Their trial continued over two Assizes and the pair were condemned to death but it seems that the sentence was commuted.

Richard and William Raisin, and another man, Thomas

Withington, were charged at Penkridge with assaulting Zachariah Smith at The Hattons in 1864. There was insufficient evidence against Withington but the Raisens, who were both aged about 18, were found guilty; William paid a fine and costs of £1, whereas Richard, who had kicked the victim in the head while he was on the ground, was fined double. Not having the means to pay, he was sentenced to six weeks with hard labour.

Fifteen years later, Richard Raisen, who worked as a farm labourer, got more than he bargained for when he crossed Emma Corser. He came to her house in a drunken state and asked her to 'turn out' her husband, something to which she objected. As she stood in the doorway, Raisin struck her with a stick, but she wrested it from him and hit him several times, knocking him to the ground. She went directly to the Police Station to show the mark on her hand and give the rest of the story. On this occasion, Raisin was ordered to pay 7 shillings in costs when the matter came to court.

Incidentally, entered into the 'Place of Birth' column beside Raisen's name on the 1881 census are the words "Deddly Dick" - perhaps that was his nickname or maybe he had been born on a canal boat? At the time he was living with his in-laws at Bishops Wood.

Earlier in the same year that Raisen assaulted Emma Corser, an ex-railway guard named William Lane took local constable James Mulrooney to court on a charge of assault. The Penkridge Magistrate was told that Lane was drinking in the Bridge Inn at about 5.30pm when Mulrooney came in, dressed in plain clothes. Lane alleged that Mulrooney grabbed him very firmly by the arm and not knowing who had hold of him, asked why he was being treated in this way. Mulrooney asked for his name and address and then went outside with Lane in tow. Outside Lane demanded to know the name and address of the other man and why he was being so treated.

What Lane didn't know, and Mulrooney had failed to tell him until they were outside, was that there was an ejection warrant issued against the landlord, Edward John Whitehouse, and he should not have been serving customers. Lane went to the police station on the following day to show the Sergeant his arm which was by now black and blue. At court, the landlord said he didn't see Mulrooney grab the man but other witnesses backed-up Mr Lane's account. The Constable was fined 12 shillings plus costs for his quite literally heavy-handed behaviour. The warrant referred to was obtained by William Bowles, the owner of the Bridge Inn because he and Mr Whitehouse had a disagreement about fixtures and the license. The warrant, issued in October 1888 gave Whitehouse 21 days to leave but he had not complied.

Stephen Barnes, alias Stephen Lloyd was sentenced to 4 months with hard labour for attacking Hetty Maria Walker of Engleton Mill in 1892. Miss Walker, aged 25, and her friend Miss Riley had been to a Bank Holiday flower show at Codsall and while walking from Brewood towards Engleton they noticed they were being followed by a man they had earlier seen outside a pub. The man, later identified as Barnes, made some indecent remark then grabbed Miss Walker, threw her down on the roadside bank and tried to sexually assault her. The young woman managed to fend him off until her friend was able to summon help, at which point Barnes ran off. He was arrested the next day and tried at Penkridge Police Court.

In 1895, William Upperdine, a stonemason who lived at 32 Park Lane, took his stepson to court on a charge of assault. Mr Upperdine told the court that George Bate, a former soldier, came to his house in a drunken state. When Mr Upperdine made some comment to his daughter, Bate knocked him down and threatened to kill him, saying that Upperdine had summoned him once before and he would make sure he didn't do it again. For his part, Bate said that Upperdine was always knocking his wife and daughter about and he was just standing up for them. He claimed that he had not hit the older man, but merely pushed him backwards and he had fallen on a chair. The Magistrate said that this was still technically an assault and the offence was aggravated by being carried out in the complainant's own home. Mr Bate was fined five shillings plus costs of almost twice as much.

William Daw (a 'navvy'), William Conway (a blacksmith) and several other men had been drinking at The Crown in Handsacre, near Rugeley, in May 1862. During the evening a dispute arose about a purse of money which one man had lost and which it was alleged, Daw now possessed. On being ejected from the premises at a quarter to midnight, the subject of the purse was again brought up between the men. At some point Conway announced "Clear the way, I'm going to hit you" and punched Daw violently on the forehead. As Daw was very drunk, he went down immediately and could not get to his feet for over a minute. When he managed to do so, he walked after Conway but was floored for a second time. When he finally staggered to his feet, he made his way to his former lodgings, where he remained until 4am. He then set off for his house at Hednesford, finally reaching home almost twelve hours later.

Daw was very badly bruised about the head and face and over the following days, regularly bathed his head and put butter on his face in an attempt to reduce the swelling. Although he went to work straight away, his condition deteriorated until he finally became delirious and was admitted to Brewood Workhouse. On admission he was found to be suffering from erysipelas (a bacterial infection) in the wounds on his face and he died a few days later. An inquest held at the Angel Inn, was presented with the results of the post mortem, which showed that the injuries to Daw's head and face were the cause of his death. The inquest jury decided that Conway should be tried for manslaughter and he was committed for trial at the Quarter Sessions.

At the Summer Assizes, the court heard conflicting opinions about the treatment Daw had administered to himself. Mr Gilby, the house surgeon at the Union thought that butter would not be a good remedy, whereas Mr Green, who carried out the post mortem, thought it would. For the defence, Mr Motteram told the court that there was no evidence that the blows had caused William Daw's death. After hearing three reputable character witnesses, the jury found in Conway's favour and he was acquitted.

William Butler was out walking with his dog near Brewood Hall in early July 1835 when the animal seemed to take great interest in a spot near a water-filled pit. On going to investigate, Mr Butler found the body of a newly-born baby girl.

When Mr Robinson, the parish surgeon, conducted a post mortem he could not ascertain whether the child had been born alive, but there were no marks of violence on the infant's body.

Following local investigations, Ann Lowe, a single woman aged 26, was arrested and subsequently charged at Staffordshire Assizes with concealing the birth of a child. The court heard that on 1st July, she called at the house of Elizabeth Powell at about 7am and the pair went off to their work of hay-making at Water Eaton. Ms Powell told her friend that she looked very ill and, knowing that Ann was heavily pregnant, said she was worried that she would miscarry. Ann replied that she was no more in the family way than Elizabeth. The pair worked together all day but despite looking extremely unwell and being told to go home, Ann worked on.

Ann Sampson told the court that the defendant had worked for her as a domestic servant and that on Whit Sunday she had confronted her about being pregnant. The young woman eventually admitted the fact and Mrs Sampson recommended that she go to her friend's house in Newport to "lie in" (ie to have her baby), which she did, although she returned to Brewood soon after. Mrs Sampson told the court that Lowe already had three children and that in each case they had been born at the Workhouse. Mr Robinson said he had delivered all of Miss Lowe's children and that in each case, delivery was very quick. He also told the court that he had examined the witness and confirmed that she had recently given birth. She was also, he said, "a woman of very weak intellect". When he examined her, she told him that the child had lived for about fifteen minutes and after it died she threw it into the pit.

While there was no evidence that she had done the child any harm, the court found her guilty of the charge that had been brought. The judge said he was inclined to treat her leniently and passed sentence of six weeks imprisonment but without hard labour. A woman by the name of Ann Lowe, with a four-year-old daughter, Caroline, was recorded at the Brewood workhouse six years after this event but whether or not it was the same woman is unclear.

Chapter 5
Pubs & Drink

In the nineteenth century, the public houses of Brewood were mostly clustered around Market Place; the Fleur-de-Lis on the eastern side, the Lion and Gifford Arms on the north, the Angel on the north-west and the Swan on the west. A little further away lay the Chequered Ball and the Boat Inn, both along Bargate Street, the Admiral Rodney on Dean Street and the Three Stirrups and Malt Shovel on Stafford Street. Numerous other shorter-lived pubs and beer-houses were scattered around the village at various times during the century.

In addition to their usual function, public houses frequently hosted inquests, auctions, sporting events and celebrations of every kind, as many still do; until the late nineteenth century, there were few if any public buildings that could serve these purposes in the small towns and villages of rural Staffordshire. Inns were sometimes the first resort in an emergency and many will have accommodated the injured or deceased.

It was not just pub buildings that served multiple purposes

either; very often the landlord himself would have another occupation. There are many instances in the locality of publicans also working as farmers, blacksmiths, butchers, wheelwrights and so on. For example, Edward Whitehouse of the Bridge Inn was also a butcher, Thomas Grosvenor of the Blue Bell on Watling Street, was also a farmer and market gardener.

In the middle years of the century, in addition to the established local inns, there were also several beer-houses - private dwellings licensed to sell beer but not spirits. These came into existence following an Act of 1830, which sought to increase competition and at the same time turn consumers away from gin. Public houses, which faced stricter regulation, were unhappy with this competition and the mushrooming of beer-houses increased drunkenness rather than reduced it. That said, there were controls in place upon the suitability of beer-house keepers beyond the usual weights and measures: for example, like inn-keepers, they had to pay a financial penalty if they wished to continue in business after being convicted of a felony.

There was a local case where this was enforced in 1855, when John Tart, who kept the Black Lion Inn at Slade Heath, had been found guilty of receiving stolen hay and straw. As he couldn't renew his usual license he took out a beer license, although he was still brought to court for failing to pay the requisite penalty. Legislation regarding beer-houses was gradually amended and by the end of the century, they had all but ceased to exist.

Details about some of Brewood's inns are given below, but

many are also mentioned in the following section regarding drink and in the chapters dealing with crime.

Angel Inn

In July 1834, two houses on Stafford Street, with gardens, piggeries and a "well of good water" were auctioned at the Angel Inn. The occupiers, George Davies and John Rogers would show prospective buyers around if required.

When landlord Mr Greensall decided to leave the Angel in 1838, he auctioned his possessions at the inn. The lots included:

> *Mahogany, oak and deal tables, chairs, eight capital goose feather beds, tent, four-post and other bedsteads, chest of drawers, carpeting and various chamber requisites, kitchen and scullery utensils, clock, barrels, tubs and a variety of useful goods; also, one capital 5-year old chestnut mare: an excellent roadster, fleet and steady in harness*

There was a shooting competition at the Angel on the day before New Year's Eve 1858, the prizes being a "fat pig weighing about 20 scores and a neat well-built dog-cart" - the winner to choose and the runner-up to have the other prize. Restrictions governing the amount of shot and the maximum allowed bore were stipulated and contestants for the 28 available places had to pay £1 to enter. The prize of a pig was a common feature of such contests in pubs across the county, the light cart less so.

An auction of four fields of pasture and meadow beside the Bell Inn on Watling Street was held at the Angel Inn in early December 1863. This was followed by a much larger auction on Christmas Eve of 19 lots of land, mostly at Somerford and Horsebrook.

Three Stirrups

The Three Stirrups came up for auction at the Star & Garter in Wolverhampton in September 1890. Most inns and taverns of the time were not restricted to a single building, as are the majority of pubs of today. The property, occupying about 2 acres, comprised:

> *Bar, Smoke Room, Tap Room, Club Room, Three Bedrooms, Cooking Kitchen, Cellar, Brewhouse, Dairy, Store Room, Two Stables, Shedding, Piggeries, Large Productive Garden, Croft of Land*

Five adjoining dwellings with workshops were included, the whole being said to have an excellent water supply and pump (which was probably disingenuous, given the state of the water and drainage in Stafford Street at that time!).

King's Arms

There was a public house known as the Kings Arms in Brewood in the late 1700s but the exact location is not known. In March 1772, it was the venue for the auction of a large local residence which included a malthouse, garden, stable and barn.

Malt Shovel

The Malt Shovel lay at the junction of Deansfield Road and Stafford Street, the building being most recently used as a takeaway. The inn had its own malthouse, stabling and cow-house.

In 1850, the landlord-cum-farmer Thomas Richards advertised hawthorn saplings for sale. They were much in demand for planting hedgerows at the time, as his stock of 100-150 *thousand* trees testifies.

When Mr Richards passed away around the beginning of 1864, his livestock (consisting of cows, calves, pigs, a horse and a pony), the malthouse utensils and all his household furniture was auctioned on-site.

Joseph Wells of Darlaston was the next keeper but his tenure was short – four years after he took over, the premises were once more to let. At this time, the inn and two adjoining cottages were owned by Mrs Heath of The Woolley.

A pig weighing over 32 scores (620lb or about 45 stones!) was the prize in a shooting competition held at the Malt Shovel in 1870, dwarfing that on offer at the Angel Inn mentioned earlier.

In 1890, Malt Shovel landlord James Pitchford took Isaac Moore to court claiming that he had stolen 45lbs of potatoes. The case was dismissed when the court heard that it was a case of disputed tenancy rather than a theft. A few years later, having left the Malt Shovel to farm at Hyde Mill, Mr Pitchford was once more at court. This time because his daughter Florence had been indecently assaulted by James Lewis junior of The Woolley. Lewis was fined 5s plus costs.

A couple of years later, the demise of the inn seemed to be near when there was a two-fold objection to the renewal of its license; firstly because it was falling into disrepair and secondly because there were already enough public houses in the vicinity. In the end the license was granted and the pub continued to operate well into the 20th century.

The Boat Inn was also in decline in the latter part of the century; in 1880 Joseph Ward applied for the license to be transferred to new premises at Bishop's Wood. The application was rejected and within about fifteen years the Boat had ceased to exist.

Lion Inn

The Lion, at times also known as the Red Lion seems to have been combined with the Giffard's Arms - whether they were separate but adjacent houses at one time is unclear but they certainly operated as a unit for at least part of their existence.

Over the course of the nineteenth century, the combined public houses of Brewood were used for literally thousands of auctions, with the Lion seeming to be the favourite venue. As mentioned earlier, innkeepers sometimes auctioned their own belongings on-site when they were leaving. For example, in early 1842, landlord Joseph Smith put his possessions at the two properties up for auction without reserve. The lots consisted of:

> *Excellent mahogany and oak dining*
> *Pembroke and pillar tables*
> *Neat sofa*

Imitation rosewood and other chairs
Chimney glasses
Handsome four post and tent bedsteads in moreen, chintz, and dimity furniture
Excellent feather beds, blankets and counterpanes, twelve pairs of sheets
Table and other linen
Painted washstands and dressing tables, chairs and other chamber furniture
A large quantity of cut and plain glass
Tea china, handsomely painted china dessert service
Large earthenware dinner service, plate and plated goods
Well bred sow in-pig, four capital store pigs
Cart and gearing
Part of a rick of capital hay
Worcester and Sussex hops
Home-cured bacon and hams
Patent straw engine by Brewster
Pikels, rakes and numerous other effects

In 1840, the Lion Inn was the venue for a dinner, organised by the Conservative electors of the area, to which Lord Ingestre was invited. A strictly limited number of tickets were available, only from the Inn itself, priced at 5 shillings each.

Unmarried sisters Mary and Frances Plant ran a grocery store on Bargate Street in the early 1850s and later at Market Place. Frances Plant placed an advertisement in 1853 inviting her friends to "favour her with their friendship and support" at a house-warming, to be held at the 'Lion Inn & Giffard's Arms

Hotel' on 15th September at 4pm. Tickets at 10 shillings each, to include dinner, desert and a bottle of wine.

Presumably the event was to mark their relocation to Market Place but why the advertisement has no mention of the other sister is a mystery. The Lion seems to have been used for 'house-warming' parties for some time; Henry Wright held his there in July 1842.

The Lion also hosted dinner for the opening of St Mary's church in June 1844. On this occasion tickets were substantially less, at 2s 6d a head, although wine was not included – probably a good idea as the meal was held between services!

Brook House, on the Coven Road, was auctioned at the Lion Inn on 30th January 1854. The property included:

> *"...excellent outbuildings, fold-yard, productive garden and orchard appurtenant thereto, together with six pieces or parcels of rich, arable, meadow and pasture land."*

The former occupant, who had now taken over the Angel Inn, was John Fox (not to be confused with the drunken saddler of the same name mentioned elsewhere). According to the 1851 census, Mr Fox was a farmer and 'Posthouse keeper' although Brook House had recently been a beer-house known as 'The Vauxhall'. The house and workshop of local lock-maker Joseph Lloyd was disposed of at the same sale.

In spring 1864, an auction of local properties by Aston &

Sollom of Wolverhampton was held at the Lion Inn. The lots included three houses and gardens in 'Bar Gate' and the four tenements behind them, having a total area of some 1600 square yards. Other lots included three houses with gardens, pigstys and outbuildings and three three-storey houses, all in Newport Street. The whole was said to be well supplied with water.

At this time, many properties in Brewood were still 'copyhold' (rather than 'freehold'), an ancient form of tenure that imposed manorial duties as well as certain rights on the holder, but by the end of the century, copyholding had practically disappeared.

The elegant-sounding Brewood 'Card And Dancing Assembly' held its annual meetings at the Lion Inn from at least 1831. These social gatherings seem to have originated in the middle of the Georgian era and were held at venues across the country, most often in public houses. On 10th February 1834, tickets to an event at the Lion, to include tea and supper as well as card games and dancing, were priced at 7 shillings for men, whereas ladies would be charged 2 shillings less!

Thomas Clifford had been licensee at both the Swan and the Lion during his 40 years of living in Brewood. He collapsed and died of a heart attack at his Bargate Street home in 1911.

Fleur-de-Lis Inn

A property auction at the 'Flower De Luce' (as it appeared in the advertisement) was held in November 1795. The dwelling, with outbuildings and garden:

"are situated in the most centrical and pleasant part of the town of Brewood, and are calculated for the residence of a genteel family"

No clue is provided as to the house involved, but schoolmaster Mr Carless was the man to see if you wanted to view it.

In the following year the inn distributed sale catalogues for another auction, in this case to be held at Somerford. The furniture and possessions of Mr Mason went under the hammer over two days – the second day being devoted to his large and valuable collection of books, some dating back into the 1650s.

In May 1830, the Brewood Association for the Prosecution of Felons (formed in 1819) held its annual meeting at the Fleur-de-Lis. In the days before the establishment of a nationwide police force, many towns and villages set up such associations, most often with notable figures at the helm, offering a scale of rewards for information leading to a conviction. The Brewood association, with Messrs Mockton, Richards, Brewster and Bate among their members, offered over £15 for conviction for a capital offence down to 10 shillings for the least serious crimes. These associations seemed to use a 'boiler-plate' advertisement and universal fees, as can be seen from the Penkridge association's advertisements placed in the same year.

In August 1834, another house and land were auctioned at the Fleur-de-Lis Inn. The dwelling, occupied by a Mrs Mellor, consisted of a parlour, kitchen, four bedrooms and a garden. The land, possibly adjacent to the house, consisted of two separate pastures "down Oram's Lane", totalling $8^{1/2}$ acres. Mr Smith, the publican would show the land to those who expressed an interest in advance of the auction.

Bridge Inn

An inquest was held at the Bridge Inn in May 1867, after the body of a new born child was found in the canal by the road over-bridge. The baby seemed to have been delivered at full term but, being in such a badly decomposed state, it had not been possible to determine the cause of death at the post mortem. The infant had been wrapped in black cloth, which appeared to be from the lining of a dress. Bizarrely, a baby had been discovered near the same spot and wrapped in a similar material, less than twelve months beforehand.

In 1900, William Gallimore of The Scotlands, Wolverhampton, was sentenced to a month's hard labour for stealing two coats, two vests and a pair of trousers. He took the items from a trap owned by Samuel Sharp which was standing in the yard of the Bridge Inn. Gallimore was arrested near Shifnal, wearing some of the clothes and having the rest in his possession.

Chequered Ball

Local man Henry Turner, was presented with a large 'Savory' silver soup tureen and dishes at the Chequered Ball in 1845. This valuable set, from a renowned silversmith, was given in recognition of his kindness to the poor of the parish.

The Chequered Ball was advertised for let at £13 per annum in 1857. It possessed a back garden well-stocked with fruit trees, a bowling alley and outbuildings but there was no mention at all of the state of the business or the interior of the property!

Renewal of the license for the inn was refused in 1892 because the structural alterations which had previously been stipulated had not been carried out. At that date it had been licensed for 150 years.

Swan Inn

In 1835, an auction for the 'Blue Bells near Ivetsey Bank' was held at the Swan. The pub may have been the forerunner of the present day Bell Inn, although that house is labelled simply as 'Bell' on a map of 1775 (it was one of six inns between Gailey and Ivetsey Bank at that time!). Three years later a number of houses with gardens in Newport Street were also sold by auction at the Swan.

In 1843 Francis Ray of Bargate Street decided to sell-up his malting business and he engaged auctioneers Walker & Page to dispose of his equipment and animals via a sale at the Swan Inn. Considering he was in his mid-twenties, Mr Ray, who may have been related to John Ray who ran the Swan Inn, had a considerable amount of valuable property:

> "The livestock consists of two excellent cows and calves, two very useful half-bred hackney horses, a very fast brown harness mare, promising year old colt by Balloon, a useful mare by Emancipation, a filly foal by Necromancer, and stinted to Bilboa, two well bred sows and eleven strong store pigs."

> "Also a light spring cart and harness, ladies and

gentlemans saddles and bridles, upwards of 200 bags, malt screen and malting tools, half a pocket of Sussex hops, ten flitches of home-cured bacon, ten hams and ten pairs of chawls."*

"*Also a rick of capital well-ended hay about 10 tons.*"

"*The furniture comprises useful and handsome articles for the parlour and sitting room, four post and tent bedsteads, fine feather beds, chairs, washstands and dressing tables, a handsome toilet service and other chamber furniture, useful kitchen requisites, brewing vessels, ale casks, a large stone cistern and other effects.*"

In 1845 the premises adjoining the Swan, comprising a bakehouse, butcher's shop and slaughterhouse were available to let.

In 1854, Wolverhampton auctioneer Thomas Page held an auction at the Swan Inn for five fields at Shutt Green - 'The First Rakels', 'Rakels Wood', 'Rakels Meadow', 'Little Moor Meadow' and 'Little Leasow'.

Public houses and auctioneer's premises were not always used for sales, sometimes auctions took place 'in situ' at houses, farms and other places. In 1847 for example, the late Miss Grundy's possessions including furniture, plate, linen, china, glass and other effects were auctioned at her house in Bargate Street.

---

* Pigs cheeks

A decade later six acres af turnips, three ricks of straw and clover and an assortment of farm equipment and household furniture was put up for sale at Marsh Farm (near Crateford), where Alexander Priestly needed to realise his assets because he was "under distress for rent". The Great Agricultural Depression, which began about thirty years later as a result of the availability of cheap North American grain, left farmers and their labourers all over the country in similar situations, often losing their livelihood entirely.

The possessions of Mr J. J. Robinson, a recently deceased local surgeon were auctioned at Stafford Street in 1849. The most interesting part of his estate was

> *"a very valuable and select library of books, containing about 600 volumes on general literature and about 100 volumes of medical and surgical works"*

In 1852 the furnishings and other items belonging to Mr Brewster, who had moved to Birmingham, were auctioned at his Market Place premises. There were a few interesting items among the more usual lots, including "Brussels floor carpets, an excellent patent mangle, a telescope and a magic lantern".

Ten years later, readers of the Staffordshire Advertiser were informed of an auction to be held at a house "near the canal bridge" - scant information, as even the occupier's name was omitted, but Dean's Hall Farm seems the most likely candidate. The gentleman who was "leaving Brewood" sought to dispose of furniture, feather beds, four pairs of scales and some churns.

Admiral Rodney

The 'Rodney' and two adjacent houses, occupied by Messrs Stoker and Gosling, were sold by auction at the Lion in May 1841. In an advertisement for the auction, the property, at that time run by Aaron Anslow, was described as an "old-established and well-known public house". It had its own malthouse, stabling, cow-houses and a croft of land behind. The advert continues:

> "...standing upon a square of nearly an acre, to an an enterprising purchasor offers an investment seldom to be met with. The malthouse, with every convenience, has been advantageously worked, in conjunction with the business. As a public house the 'Admiral' has maintained a character for respectability and first rate business for sixty years. Fortunes have been made and spent there; and an attentive person may soon accumulate one, by continuing the same course of industry which has characterised the present proprietor, and ensured the support of the spirited inhabitants of Brewood"

This places the opening of the inn firmly in the 1780s - George Brydges Rodney, after whom the house as named, achieved his most famous victory, over the French, in 1782. Two acres of pasture land known as 'Brickkiln Piece' and lying along Jones' Lane was sold at the same auction. It seems that Jones' Lane became known as Horsebrook Lane soon after.

The proprietor of the inn tried an interesting tack to encourage visitors in 1870. A letter was sent to the editor of the Daily Gazette in Birmingham, saying that a local gardener had obtained some eggs for hatching and that a duck and a chicken had emerged from a single egg! The egg was said to have been an unusual shape and colour but the two birds were perfectly healthy and resembled each other in colour, being black with white-tipped feathers. Anyone interested in seeing this freak of nature and verifying the account for themselves, was exhorted to visit the inn.

Drink

Although beer in Victorian Britain was somewhat weaker than it is today, many working class men thought that eight pints could be safely consumed before becoming intoxicated. It is unsurprising then, that court reports for almost any week in the nineteenth century show that Brewood, like virtually every other village and town in the land, was plagued by drunken behaviour. The offences were usually minor and sometimes have a humorous side when viewed from this distance in time, but occasionally they were associated with more serious offences such as fighting or assaulting police officers.

For misdemeanours at the lower end of the scale, transgressors usually ended up with a fine of a few shillings, with progressively higher tariffs, sometimes including imprisonment, for infractions of a more serious nature. Given the number of public houses available within a small radius, the 'one over the eight' mentality and the comparatively low price of beer, it is hardly surprising that drunkenness was rife.

Although drunkenness amongst women might seem to be a new phenomenon, especially in town and city centres, it was just as common during the 1800s. Perhaps the most surprising thing is that cases from the past do not just concern younger women, there are plenty of examples of women right up to their 70s being just as reckless, although some of these were habitual heavy drinkers rather than one-off binge drinkers.

William Taylor and Thomas Hipwood, labourers of Kiddemore Green, were accused at Penkridge Police Court of being drunk and fighting in Bargate Street in January 1884. They called a witness who stated that they had both had a drink although they were not drunk but PC McCabe begged to differ. Neither of them denied the fact that they were fighting and a fine of 10s 9d was duly issued.

Two months later, labourer Henry Jones was fined for being drunk in Market Place, and Thomas Smith, a painter of Shop Lane, for being drunk in Stafford Street. Both were fined 15 shillings by the Magistrate at Penkridge, constables McCabe and Spendlove providing the necessary evidence.

Another typical hearing at Penkridge in 1890 resulted in fines for Thomas Bryan, William Weller and Thomas Welch, all of whom were drunk in Market Place on different days. At the same session, Brewood men Joseph Hawkins and George Biddle at least offered something a little different - they were fined for negligent driving (of a horse and cart) at Coven.

'Eliza Hiles' was fined 18 shillings for being drunk and disorderly in Market Square on 6th January 1888. Constable Lawton told Penkridge Police court that she was creating a huge disturbance and witness John MacDermott said she was making "a great noise". The name of the defendant reported in the Lichfield Mercury was probably a mistake; it was most likely Eliza Holles, a widowed farmer's wife of Horsebrook.

Later that same year Joseph Morris was also fined for making a noise, but this time inside the Lion Inn, the noise being a tirade of abuse aimed at his wife! The landlord, Mary Ann Summers, asked him to leave but he refused to go. The Penkridge Magistrate fined him 10 shillings plus the same in costs.

In July, the Lichfield Mercury couldn't resist a pun in their short report about a local drunk; the paragraph was entitled "Drinking Too Much Of What Is 'Brewed'". It related to labourer George Perry, who was found lying in Horsebrook Lane at 10.45pm.

In December Thomas Duffey was charged with two offences; refusing to quit and breaking a window. The landlord of the Chequered Ball, Charles Clarke, told Penkridge Petty Sessions that Duffey was in an excited state when he entered the premises although he couldn't say whether it was because he was already drunk. He wasn't served with any drink but soon became abusive and Mr Clarke sent for the police. In the meantime Duffey left the premises but returned later, and finding the door locked, picked up several stones and threw them at the pub, breaking a window. In his defense, Duffey claimed that Clarke had struck him with a truncheon. A witness, George Taylor, confirmed this, saying Clarke went upstairs to get the truncheon then came down and struck Duffey with it. The Bench was unimpressed with Duffey's defense and he was ordered to pay a total of £1 14s 6d in damages, fine and costs.

John Etheridge, a draper's assistant of High Green, and his wife Sarah Ann, appeared at Tamworth Police court in 1898 charged with being drunk and disorderly at Hopwas. Mr Etheridge had been working at the barracks nearby but remained in lodgings in the area for another week or so after completing his work. On a Saturday afternoon, he and his wife were invited back to the barracks for drinks but the pair clearly over-indulged. They returned to his lodgings in the late evening only to find that they were no longer available, so the couple set off in the direction of Whittington. At about 11pm, a local policeman heard a disturbance and when he went to investigate, he came across Mr Etheridge who claimed that a group of soldiers had abducted his wife. Walking a little further, the officer found Mrs Etheridge with the men but as he approached they ran away. When Mr Etheridge finally came up, he inexplicably hit his wife!

Constable Finney told the court that husband and wife were both drunk; Mrs Etheridge being so bad that she had to be put in a cab to convey her to the police station. Mr Etheridge said he had hit his wife because he was over-excited and didn't know what he was doing. His wife deposed that she was not drunk at all, just very tired. The couple escaped a fine but the Bench ordered them to pay costs of 12s 6d.

Another Brewood couple, James and Ada Anderson, were charged with being drunk in a public place in January 1899, this time closer to home. Constable Tytherleigh told the Police Court at Penkridge that he saw Mrs Anderson sat on a doorstep in a very drunken state, surrounded by a group of people. Her husband who was in a similar condition came up and took off his jacket, spoiling for a fight but the constable took him into custody and locked him up at the Police Station. Later in the day he came across Mrs Anderson once more and she was so drunk that he arranged to have her taken home in a cart. The Andersons were fined 13s 6d for their drunken behaviour.

In 1889, a local stone-cutter, William Taylor was charged with being drunk whilst in charge of a horse and cart. A witness, William Cartwright, deposed that he had seen the accused trying to get hold of the reins of his cart in Lapley Road and while leaning forward, fell off the vehicle. Taylor was fined a total of 19 shillings including costs.

Thomas Flemming was jailed for four months for violently assaulting his wife at their home on Stafford Street in 1892. Margaret Flemming was a heavy drinker and was inebriated when she returned to their house one day in July 1892 at 2.30pm. Her husband began to abuse her and then ordered her out of the house. When she refused to leave he locked all the doors and assaulted her but when she cried out "murder", someone came to the front door and Mr Flemming ran away.

In the late afternoon, Mrs Flemming went out with a neighbour, returning at about 7.30pm. At about 10.30pm Constable Whitehurst heard screams of "murder" from the house and when he went to investigate found the door locked. Looking through the keyhole, he saw Mr Flemming kicking his wife in the head as she lay on the floor. The officer called out for Flemming to desist but had to break open the door to finally stop him. P.C. Whitehurst told Cannock Petty Sessions that husband and wife were both using bad language when he took Mr Flemming into custody. In his defense, Flemming claimed that his wife was so drunk that he was trying to pick her up off the floor and carry her to bed! Margaret Flemming told the court that she wanted a separation order, which was duly granted.

Sergeant Whitehurst looked in at the Swan Inn a few days before Christmas 1894 and found farm labourer James Murphy drunk in the passage. Arthur Lowder, the landlord, was also there, trying to persuade Murphy to leave the premises and between the two he was soon ejected. Mr Lowder told the Penkridge Petty Sessions that Murphy was already drunk when he entered the Inn and asked for a pint of whiskey. A fine of three shillings including costs was imposed.

Joseph Fox, of Dean Street, mentioned elsewhere, was a neighbour of Enoch Plant (also mentioned elsewhere) and was another prodigious drinker who frequently ended up in court and seemed to spend as much on fines as he did on beer. The last decade of his drunken career (so to speak) offers ample illustration of his exploits.

In 1890, already having a string of convictions, he was fined 20 shillings plus costs and sent to prison for 7 days following an incident in Dean Street. Constable Hewitt found Fox shouting at the top of his voice, speaking against the bible and clergymen to a crowd of people. The officer escorted Fox to his house but he continued his discourse from his bedroom window. Fox told the court at Penkridge that the last time he was convicted he had signed 'the pledge' (i.e. agreed not to drink) for 3 months and this most recent event took place three days after that period had expired. He offered the court an unfathomable explanation for his "preaching" on the night in question - it was because he "felt almost prostrate with being tee-total"!

In 1892 he was found guilty of being drunk and disorderly and using foul language on two separate occasions, being fined 10 shillings for each offence.

In 1894, William Bakewell, the landlord of the Admiral Rodney was prosecuted for serving Fox when he was already drunk. Constable Burton saw Fox enter the premises in a drunken state and found he had been served with a pint of ale shortly afterwards. At court, Bakewell claimed that Fox didn't appear to be drunk and had told him that he was buying the beer for a neighbour. He said he had ejected Fox from the premises on 20 or more previous occasions rather than have any trouble with him. Bakewell was fined £5 but fortunately for him, his license was not endorsed. Fox was fined 10 shillings plus costs or 14 days in jail in default.

Mr Fox was tried in his absence in May of the last year of the century - when he was just under 70 years of age - for being drunk and disorderly in Stafford Street. It was about the 60th time he had been up on such a charge and the second time that year. Lord Hatherton had clearly had enough of the man; he told the court that if he saw Fox again he would have him committed to a home for inebriates. As it was, he once more imposed a fine of 10 shillings plus costs. Surely enough, four months later Fox was back before the same court, although he once again escaped with a fine, this time of 29 shillings in total. Fanny Donlon (mentioned elsewhere) was fined a total of 14 shillings for being drunk and disorderly at the same sessions.

In September of the following year the inevitable happened;

Fox was charged with being drunk on two occasions, in Market Place and Newport Street, and using abusive language. He received 7 days with hard labour for each offence, the sentences to run concurrently.

As Lord Hatherton had warned, he was then charged with being an habitual drunkard. By way of evidence, Sergeant Tytherleigh deposed that he had been in court on numerous occasions when Fox had been convicted in the past. The court head that Mr Fox was usually given food instead of money because people knew that if he had cash he would spend it on drink. He was committed to the Victoria Homes at Brentry, near Bristol, for two years.

Thomas Linskey, a farm labourer in his mid-30s who lived on Stafford Street, was fined over a pound for two drunk and disorderly offences at the same hearing. If he was privy to Joseph Fox's case, it may have provided a salutary warning about his future conduct.

Margaret Hemming of School Lane (as it seems to have been known at the time) was fined 10 shillings including costs for being drunk in August 1895. Sergeant Whitehurst saw her being led out of the Admiral Rodney yard by her friend Annie Barlow at 7.20 in the evening. She fell over but was helped to her feet by her friend and eventually collected by her brother. Ms Barlow told the Penkridge court that her friend had drunk nothing in the half hour she had been at the pub, except some spirits given to her by a man named Hall, after which she fainted and had to be brought-to by the landlady using a glass of soda water.

The following year, married woman Emma Dodd was fined for being "drunk on the highway" and was fined a shilling plus costs. At the same hearing, villagers George Perry and Thomas Welsh were also fined for drunkenness.

Two years before the Great War, another woman was fined for drunk and disorderly behaviour - this time it was a Mrs Henshaw who was creating a disturbance in Stafford Street at 10:30pm. On hearing the racket, Constable Wood went to the spot and tried to persuade the woman to go home but before long her husband came to collect her. Despite this, she continued to rail until after midnight. She was fined 2 shillings in her absence at Penkridge.

Chapter 6
Shops, Property, Workhouse & Health

Shops & Property

In the Victorian era, a whole series of efforts were made to protect and improve public health and safety, both at home and at work. In addition, much legislation was enacted to safeguard the travelling public and to reduce many forms of exploitation. To ensure that these laws were being complied with, a range of different officers were appointed, both locally and nationwide. There were separate inspectors for factories, mines, railways, education, roads, tax, lighting and a dozen other things.

The first nationwide Weights and Measures Inspectors were appointed in the 1880s, before that time it was the Inspector of Nuisances, the local Constable or parish appointed inspectors who would look into matters of unfair trading or adulterated food.

In August 1862, a number of local publicans and traders were fined for having measures that were detrimental to their customers. Appearing at the Petty Sessions, Thomas Buckley of the Harrows at Coven and Thomas Smith of the Spread Eagle at Gailey were each fined for having under-sized glasses, cups and jugs. Brewood baker Mary Mills, and grocer Charles Austin, both had scales that disadvantaged their customers.

In the following year, Joseph Green was fined 2s 6d plus costs for using unstamped measures at his malthouse. Mr Green, who was then in his sixties, farmed over 70 acres and had a malthouse on Orams Lane. The Petty Sessions heard that the two measures were quite accurate; Mr Green was not trying to defraud his customers, he had simply neglected to obtain officially approved equipment.

Thomas Shemmilt, farmer at The Hyde, was fined over £4 including costs in 1865, for possessing a sheep which was unfit for human consumption. In his defense it was said that sheep suffered badly from apoplexy in hot weather and this animal, being so affected, had to be killed. Unfortunately for Mr Shemmilt it was not disposed of in a timely manner and came to the attention of the local inspector.

Judging by the clusters of cases, it seems that weights and measures inspectors visited all of the businesses in an area for routine checks, rather than waiting until a complaint was made. In September 1885 for example, there were prosecutions of businesses in Brewood, Coven and Penkridge. At Brewood, maltster William Lees of Bargate Street was found to have unjust weights and was fined 16s 6d. Frederick Wassell, a coal dealer of Church Road, had a balance that was some 16 lbs against the customer, although he claimed he had never used that particular scale as he had others at his premises. He was fined 20 shillings and sixpence. In the last year of the century, the Wharf Manager and coal dealer, Henry Morris, was fined 10 shillings plus costs for selling coal without using any scales at all!

Thomas Allcock of Kiddemore Green was a baker who sold bread and other groceries from his cart. In 1888 he fell foul of the law when he was spotted selling bread near his home without having the required scales and weights to hand. Penkridge Police Court imposed a fine and costs totalling 13 shillings.

Golden Syrup, which came onto the market in the last 15 years of the nineteenth century, is not usually mentioned amongst the adulterated foods of that era. However, William Perkins was prosecuted for selling a 2lb tin of it, from his Church Road shop. County Inspector Mr Van Tromp, told Penkridge Police Court that the fake syrup contained 50% glucose, and while that in itself was not dangerous, it was far less expensive than the cane sugar syrup which the product was supposed to contain. The cheap syrup had been put into a 'Crosfield & Co.' branded tin which, Mr Perkins claimed he had bought in good faith from a wholesaler in Wolverhampton. Lord Hatherton, imposing a fine of £10 plus costs, said he wanted to put a stop to "this kind of fraud which affected the poor".

Mr Mills, the Surveyor of Highways at Brewood in 1850, took William Riddings of Walsall to court to recover costs in respect of the upkeep of his cow! Mr Ridding had purchased the cow from George Harris at Wolverhampton Market for £10. Within a few weeks the cow had a calf and shortly afterwards became diseased. Being assured by several cattle dealers that an ancient law entitled him to return the beast as it had become ill within three months of purchase, Riddings sent the animal back to Mr Harris at Brewood. Mr Harris was away at the time and when he came back to find the cow in his yard, he simply turned it out onto the road, from where it was recovered and accommodated by Mr Mills. At Wolverhampton Police Court, the magistrate decided that Ridding was responsible and he was fined one pound and sixpence. The cow was believed to be worth 10 shillings at most; whether it was ever returned to its rightful owner is not recorded.

Henry Robinson, a maltster of Sandy Lane was charged with non-payment of 'malt duty' by officers of the Inland Revenue at Penkridge in 1855 - he owed the substantial sum of £692. Mr Robinson offered a guilty plea but being bankrupt he was not able to pay immediately. As the law allowed, the officers were then issued with a warrant which allowed them to double the duty, although they said that they only intended to collect the original sum.

Shops and businesses changed hands in the past just as they still do today. Some were disposed of due to the retirement, death or illness of the proprietor, whereas others may have been off-loaded because they were failing or the owners credibility had been damaged. An example is provided by the drapery business in Market Place which seems to have been sold or let on many occasions during the nineteenth century. In 1835, James Farmer decided to give up the business and auctioned all of his stock, which included ironmongery. In 1848, Mr Wood sought a tenant for the shop, his advertisement describing the business as "established as a linen and woollen drapery concern for a long period, and now fitted up with every convenience for carrying on the same".

Sixteen years later the business was back on the market, this time advertised by Edward Beetlestone, who seemed to have been trying a different ancillary business to ironmongery:

> *"To be let, with immediate possession, a dwelling-house, shop and premises, situate in the Market Place, Brewood, and in which an excellent business in the Grocery and Drapery trade has for many years been carried on. The premises are well situated, and are replete with every convenience for residence; and the warehouse room is adequate to the carrying on of an extensive business."*

Mr Beetlestone also owned two residential properties in Brewood in the 1850s – a five-bedroom house with a stable and offices in Stafford Street, occupied by a Miss Kitchen, and a cottage at Hockerhill, said to have a large garden "well stocked with choice fruit trees".

Just two years after letting the drapery shop, Beetlestone had it on the market again, the existing tenant, Miss Crane having obviously failed to make a go of it. Rent was set at £30 per annum. He also had another house to let in Brewood, at £12 per annum but the address is not given.

Three Stafford Street shops with living accommodation, a stable and gardens were put up for sale at the end of 1832. A Miss Trevett, James Knibb and John Purchase were in occupation at the time; presumably they were trading from the premises but it is not clear whether their tenancy would be affected by the sale:

> *"The above premises are conveniently situated, and well calculated for carrying on an extensive trade, and are now in excellent repair"*

Interested parties were asked to apply to local solicitor Mr H Turner.

When Francis Monkton came of age in 1865, quite a few column inches were devoted to the subject in those newspapers with local concerns. However, Benjamin Bourne of Lodge Bank, Newport was less enthusiastic and he wrote to the Staffordshire Advertiser in May to complain about the legitimacy of the Monckton's claim to the Somerford Estate. According to Mr Bourne, his ancestor Robert Barbor, who died in 1761, settled the estate to the Barbor line for ever. He stated that part of the same will was being tried at Chancery at that moment, but his claim was clearly rejected.

Oakley House was also available to let in the same year that Francis Monckton reached the age of 21 and it is interesting to read the description of the property at that time:

> *Oakley House, one mile from Brewood, containing kitchen, breakfast and drawing rooms, seven bedrooms and two kitchens, detached brewhouse with laundry over, very compact courtyard with large carriage house, two stables, two loose boxes, harness room and dog house, beautiful pleasure*

gardens with ornamental lake, rustic bridge, boat and summer house, large kitchen garden, orchard and a good pew in Brewood church.

The house was said to have a Post Office nearby, be within 30 minutes by carriage of both the London North Western and Great Western Railways and to be at the centre of the Albrighton Hunt. The asking price was £50 per annum!

A house near the newly built Catholic church was available to let in 1844, applications to be made to Charles Green (the chemist referred to elsewhere), the son of Joseph Green who farmed at 'Deans Lane'. In addition to the usual rooms, it came with:

> *"...three attics, excellent dairy, pantry and china closets, and good cellaring, with pump in an enclosed yard, stable for 2 or 3 horses, granary, cow sheds for 6 cows, gig-house and piggeries with excellent garden."*

A "commodious house" situated near the church and recently occupied by Mr Hay, was available to let in the following year. It possessed:

> *"Two very agreeable parlours, convenient kitchen and brewhouse, six bed-rooms, with a store room and excellent cellaring. There is a good two-stalled stable, with a convenient gig-house, and a capital walled garden, with a choice collection of fruit trees"*

In 1891 the privately owned Brewood Gasworks was put up for auction, the owner deciding to give up the business after suffering two serious accidents. The premises, 7,000 cubic foot gasometer and the mains beneath the town were offered for sale at the Star & Garter in Wolverhampton. Only having managed to achieve a miserable £725, the lot was withdrawn.

Disputes over property boundaries have gone on since time immemorial, often over just a few inches of land. In 1883 trouble flared up between locksmith Thomas Haynes of The Pinfold, High Green, and his new neighbour James Alfred Cummings. Mr Cummings decided to build a new wall around his property but some of it encroached upon the property Mr Haynes was occupying. He informed his landlady and she immediately arranged for the new wall to be demolished, doubtless to Mr Cummings displeasure.

Some six weeks later the matter came to court, with Mr Haynes alleging that Mr Cummings had threatened him with physical violence after the wall was taken down. Mr Haynes told the court that early one morning about a fortnight earlier, he heard a noise at the front of his property and when he went to the door found that Cummings was stacking up the bricks. Haynes said "I do not allow you to throw down bricks on my thoroughfare", at which he alleged that Cummings came towards him holding up a brick and said "I will break your head with this". Mr Haynes, who was sixty-two, feared for his safety and quickly closed his door, while Cummings continued "If you come outside you will see what I will do for you".

In his defence, Cummings said that he was near a stack of bricks on his property, 12 feet from Haynes' door when the alleged threat took place. He told the court that he actually said "If you remove these bricks, I will remove you" but would not have said it if he had not been goaded by Mr Haynes. In the end the Bench believed that Mr Cummings did not pose a serious threat to Mr Haynes and the case was dismissed.

Workhouse

For those down on their luck and with no other means of support, the poor laws and the workhouse provided a buffer against utter destitution. Inmates were segregated by gender and made to work for their keep, unless they were so ill that they were lodged in the infirmary. It was not uncommon for seasonal workers, children of the poor and single mothers to be in and out of the workhouse over several years.

The Bargate Street workhouse, built around the beginning of the century, was enlarged after the establishment of the Penkridge Poor Law Union in the late 1830s and aided many poor folk for over three decades. An earlier workhouse in the vicinity was converted to residential use and served that purpose until the middle of the century.

Frederick Green, governor of the workhouse in 1830, must have been quite a character and a physically capable man. He made a bizarre £10 wager that he could kill, skin and dress eight pigs in less than four hours. He was to have no assistance other than hot water conveyed to the 'scalding tub', and the use of a winch to lift the animals from it. The pigs weighed between 240 and 300lbs each. He accomplished the feat just five minutes inside the allotted time but there is no indication who, if anyone, took him up on the bet.

In 1838, a new schoolmistress and chaplain were sought for the workhouse and in 1847 a new nurse to look after the sick was required. The advertisement for the latter specified that the ideal candidate would be a middle-aged woman, and the salary would be fourteen pounds per annum plus accommodation and food. An interview before the Board of Guardians and references would be required.

In 1851 Samuel Bowdler and his wife Mary were Governor and Matron of the workhouse, while Elizabeth Alsop was the nurse and Mary Bradshaw the schoolmistress. When the census was taken in that year, the building housed just over a hundred people ranging in age from 1 to 90, with roughly equal numbers of males and females and almost a third being children. The majority of the men were out of work agricultural labourers although a few had other occupations, such as a butcher and a brickmaker.

A little under twenty years later, the workhouse population was still around the 100 mark but it was also providing outdoor relief to about 150 vagrants per week, a figure which the Guardians felt was unsustainable. Very soon after, the Union built a new workhouse with twice the capacity at Cannock and that at Brewood was closed.

Tenders were regularly invited for the supply of provisions etc to the Workhouse, and for the supply of bread to the 'out-poor' - those parishioners to whom outdoor relief was provided at 'relieving stations'. The list of foods required in 1863 was:

> *Bread, of best seconds flour, in 4lb loaves, after being drawn from the oven 24 hours, at -- per loaf*

Best seconds flour, at -- per sack of 224lbs
Beds, rounds and stickings of beef (in equal proportions) and suet at -- per lb
Cheese, tea, sugar, yellow soap, good salted butter, treacle, dip candles, tobacco, blue and starch each at -- per lb
Oatmeal at -- per load of 240lbs
White peas at -- per bushel of 32 quarts
Rice, salt and soda at -- per cwt
Skimmed milk at -- per gallon
Potatoes at -- per bag of 180lbs net
Ale at -- per kilderkin* of 18 gallons
Port, wine, brandy and gin at -- per gallon

We should remember that all of the alcoholic items were regularly prescribed by doctors at that time - a diet of beef, ale, port and wine was often prescribed for those recovering from serious illness.

The supply of other items was also contracted out - an advertisement placed by the Newport Union at the same time as the one for Brewood mentioned above, invited tenders for "clothes, coal, hats, candles, yarn, bonnets, tailoring and coffins"

At least at Christmas, inmates had cause to celebrate as they were usually treated to a seasonal meal and more. In 1865 for example, roast beef and plum pudding was served, the adults were given pipes and tobacco while the children were given oranges. On the Monday following New Year's Day, the children were given toys and more oranges by Mrs Lonsdale of

---

*   Half a barrel

Somerford Hall. Exactly the same fare was provided at Lord Hatherton's expense in 1870. Later that year, John Austin of Standeford Mill, who was a long-serving guardian at the workhouse, passed away and his role was taken by William Chambley of The Beeches, Coven.

The Poor Rate, a local tax used to provide relief to the poor of the parish was collected by individuals appointed by the relevant union. In 1846 the Penkridge Union advertised for two Poor Rate Collectors, one in Penkridge and one in Brewood:

> *The person appointed must be competent in accounts and must reside in their respective districts. They must undertake to give one month's notice previous to resigning their offices, or forfeit one month's salary; and they must each give a bond in £300, with two sufficient sureties for the due and faithful discharge of the duties of their respective offices. Each office must further undertake to discharge the duties of an Assistant Overseer in any parish or parishes of his district in which he may be appointed to that office, without any additional salary or emolument. The salaries of the collectors will be, for the Brewood District seventy eight pounds yearly and for the Penkridge District seventy two pounds yearly.*

In 1876, a number of Brewood residents found themselves summonsed to appear at Cannock Police Court because they had failed to pay their dues. Their argument was that the late Poor Rate Collector was asking for an amount that did not correspond with that signed-off for by the magistrate and they feared that they would have to pay again as a result. While the Bench sympathised with this fact, the proper course of action was to have paid and then made an appeal. The case ended with John Ray, John Tollfree, Sarah Beech and others agreeing to pay the requisite amounts of between £4 and £20.

In addition to those who were destitute through no fault of their own, the Workhouse sometimes ended up supporting the feckless and those who sought to exploit the system. Some duped the Workhouse into providing accommodation while spending money on drink, others stole from the Union itself or exploited inmates and some used it as a place to dump their family, rather than have to support them.

John Brown stole clothing from the Brewood Workhouse in 1817 – he confessed to the crime and was publicly whipped by order of the Stafford Magistrate – while Samuel Ward was sent to the house of correction for three months for stealing from the Workhouse in 1842. He also stole clothes owned by the Union; he was wearing them when he absconded.

Brewood labourer William Hoskins, who also went by the name Austins, was brought to court in 1885 for neglecting his wife and family, who had become dependant upon the Union. An order had previously been made against him for their maintenance in the Workhouse, but after paying for a few weeks he stopped contributing. The magistrates told Hoskins he would be discharged if he took his family out of the Workhouse before the next meeting of the Board of Guardians, otherwise he would be sent to prison.

Henry and Sarah Wright were each charged with being drunk

in the village in 1889; they were seen by two different police officers, in School Road and Shop Lane, and both constables noted that they were completely intoxicated. Six years later Sarah Wright, now in her mid-60s, was once again charged with being drunk but by then she was an inmate of the Workhouse. Answering the charge at Cannock Petty Sessions, Mrs Wright said that she could remember nothing at all about the incident. Fortunately Sergeant Whitehouse was able to prove the misdemeanor. Mrs Wright promised that she would remain in the workhouse in future and with this in mind, the case was adjourned for three months. The magistrate told her that if she failed to keep her word, she would face a fine of 10 shillings plus costs when the case was reconvened. We can imagine that the Guardians were not too pleased with Mrs Wright being accommodated at their expense and yet having the means to get drunk in the evening!

Health

In autumn 1903, around fifty cases of ptomaine (food) poisoning were recorded in Brewood, although all the individuals affected eventually recovered. Amongst those affected were the village chemist, and Headmaster John Brodie, the later being so ill that there were fears for his life. The source of the illness was believed to be potted brawn, a loaf of jellied meat, sold by a local grocer. While the shopkeeper denied that the meat was the source of the outbreak, it was noted that in several families, only the individuals who had consumed the loaf fell ill.

The 'Inspector of Nuisances', (an ancient office and forerunner of the Sanitary Inspector, Public Heath Inspector and finally

Environmental Health Officer) was appointed by the parish or council and tasked with investigating all forms of nuisance, whether caused by noise, refuse, smoke, encroachment, obstruction, overcrowding, dangerous dogs or a hundred other things.

Laws to combat overcrowding came into place in the latter part of the nineteenth century and were enforced even away from towns and cities, which most people associate with slum conditions. In an attempt to minimize the spread of disease, the rules even specified the volume of air required by each person sleeping at a given dwelling - 300 cubic feet of air per person being the stipulated figure.

In October 1901, the Sanitary Inspector served an order on Fanny Donlan to abate a nuisance - she had eight people sleeping at her Stafford Street home, when the maximum permitted by law was five. She had clearly been in breach of the regulations for some time; there were five family members and two others listed at the address in the census taken earlier that year. This was not the first time the Donlans had been prosecuted - farm worker Thomas Donlan, had previously been fined for not sending one of their children to school on a regular basis. Sixpence with over four shillings in costs was the tariff imposed by Penkridge Police court in that instance.

In addition to clean air, uncontaminated drinking water is also essential to a healthy existence. As local wells in Brewood were not deep and drains had grown in an ad hoc fashion rather than being part of a unified sewerage system, there was always the possibility of domestic sewage or effluent from roads or farms entering the water supply.

In September 1849 both the Brewood Races and the Wake were suspended as a precautionary measure in view of the incidences of Cholera in the area. The suspension was unanimously recommended by the Board of Guardians of the Penkridge Union as there had been a number of fatalities from the disease, although it did not appear to be spreading. The Union had established a Committee of Health which set about implementing preventative measures by visiting houses in Brewood, Bushbury and Lapley where many cases of diarrhoea had been reported.

During a summer storm in 1898, Newport Street was flooded to a depth of 18 inches and properties in Bargate Street were badly damaged. The Surveyor told a meeting of Cannock District Rural Council that defective drainage was a major factor in the flood. In the following year there was a fatal case of typhoid in Stafford Street. 'The Inspector of Nuisances' analysed water from wells in the nearby houses and found them to be contaminated with sewage and unfit for drinking. His report found the existing sewerage system to be poorly constructed, with different sized pipes and connections which were not water-tight. He concluded that the time was right for a new system to be installed.

Putting his trust in the Lord rather than those who strove to improve public health however, the Reverend Huffadine thought the report was over-blown and that as Brewood was in decline it would be unfair to burden rate-payers with additional expense. As so often happens with public bodies when action is required, the matter was deferred. In the same year there were cases of diphtheria at Bishops Wood, where the drainage and water supply were also unsatisfactory. In one case a drain was found to run directly beneath the floorboards of a house! At least some action was taken in this instance – the school was closed immediately, the aforementioned drain was re-routed and the water supply investigated.

A report into the town's drainage system finally materialised in June 1900 and was presented to the District Council at Cannock. It calculated that the total cost of funding the works plus a system to deal with the sewage collected from the 1,400 residents, would be just shy of £4,000. If the amount were borrowed from the Public Works Loan Board, it would cost £140 per annum which would be met by $2^{1/4}$d rate. A special committee was appointed to look into the matter and the Parish Council again discussed the water supply but action was put off until pollution of the local wells had been investigated further. In the end, a complete, water-tight sewer system was not in place until the closing years of the decade, despite an Order to deal with the issue being made some forty years earlier.

Regardless of the many diseases that people of the era were exposed to, the air and water in Brewood obviously suited Amos Jenks, who died in 1893, just a couple of months short of his 104th birthday. Jenks had served in the Peninsular War and at Waterloo, seen the jubilees of King George III and Queen Victoria and retained physical and mental fitness until the end of his life - at the age of 100 he walked 10 miles to Hednesford and a week or two later walked back. His working life was spent as an agricultural labourer and later a brick-maker and he lived at Hyde Mill Lane for many decades.

An event in the middle of Mr Jenks' life shows how crime and punishment were much harsher than today. A local boy,

Thomas Picken, was prosecuted by Mr Jenks for stealing his shovel, a misdemeanour which the Wolverhampton Magistrate felt warranted three months imprisonment with hard labour and a whipping.

Even when fresh air, a healthy diet and clean water are available, there is no guarantee that everyone will benefit from them. In 1843, George Jones was imprisoned for two months for neglecting his wife. Mr Jones, aged about 45, lived with his wife Lucy at Market Place, but since their marriage she had suffered some cataclysmic mental illness and as a consequence had spent time in a lunatic asylum.

When the case was eventually brought to court, it was revealed that Mrs Jones condition had come to the attention of the parish authorities and Constable John Marsh had been asked to visit the house to ascertain the details. When directed to the upstairs room in which Mrs Jones was kept he was met by a scene of total squalor. The poor woman, completely deprived of reason, lay on a straw mattress, with some bed-clothes and an old cloak thrown over her. The room was in a disgusting state and the stench from faeces that had been allowed to build-up was insufferably offensive.

P.C. Marsh insisted that the room be cleaned and when he next visited the house a few days later this had been done. However, despite visits over succeeding weeks, the room was gradually allowed to deteriorate again. When the officer called for a fourth time, he found that it was in as bad a condition as when he first saw it. On this occasion he was accompanied by Constable William Tart, who directed Mrs Jones' sister, Elizabeth Smith, to examine the woman. She was found to be in a pitiful condition with her lower body covered in excrement. Elizabeth Ash, 20 years younger than George Jones and living with him as his wife, told the two constables that she would do nothing more for Mrs Jones.

Mrs Smith told the court that her sister was a lunatic and after leaving the asylum had lived with her (Mrs Smith's) daughter, who was paid 4 shillings a week to look after her. She stayed there for nine weeks before being taken back home by Mr Jones. After a few days at home she was sent to live with Mrs Smith, an allowance again being paid by Jones, and remained there for three years. Mrs Smith told the court that her sister was sometimes violent and that George Jones had been 'sold up' as he was no longer able to pay his rent. Mrs Smith's daughter, Elizabeth Yates, stated that she had called at Jones' house twice recently, asking to be allowed to see her aunt but on both occasions she was refused. The jury found George Jones guilty as charged, but in view of his poverty, the sentence was reduced to two months imprisonment.

References

Chapter 1

Brewood Races
Wolverhampton Chronicle and Staffordshire Advertiser 24 September 1834
Staffordshire Advertiser 30 September 1837
Wolverhampton Chronicle and Staffordshire Advertiser 30 September 1835
Staffordshire Advertiser 1 October 1836
Staffordshire Advertiser 14 September 1839
Staffordshire Advertiser 2 October 1847
Staffordshire Advertiser 3 January 1852
Wolverhampton Chronicle and Staffordshire Advertiser 31 March 1858
Yorkshire Gazette 27 December 1845
Shrewsbury Chronicle 30 March 1860

Weddings, Shows & Sports
Staffordshire Advertiser 07 July 1838
Sheffield Independent 16 November 1850
Staffordshire Advertiser 7 March 1863
Wolverhampton Chronicle and Staffordshire Advertiser 18 March 1863

Wolverhampton Chronicle and Staffordshire Advertiser 7 June 1865
RG10 Piece number 2922 Folio 33 Page 13
Wolverhampton Chronicle and Staffordshire Advertiser 4 April 1849
Lichfield Mercury 26 February 1886
Lichfield Mercury 30 June 1899
Aris's Birmingham Gazette 10 April 1869
Staffordshire Advertiser 28 September 1867
Wolverhampton Chronicle and Staffordshire Advertiser 9 February 1859
Lichfield Mercury 6 September 1901
Wolverhampton Chronicle and Staffordshire Advertiser 10 May 1843
Wolverhampton Chronicle and Staffordshire Advertiser 2 June 1847
Wolverhampton Chronicle and Staffordshire Advertiser 18 June 1856
Staffordshire Advertiser 16 July 1853

Chapter 2

Fire
Staffordshire Advertiser 2 October 1852
Wolverhampton Chronicle and Staffordshire Advertiser 19 September 1860
Staffordshire Advertiser 20 March 1830
Wolverhampton Chronicle and Staffordshire Advertiser 6 December 1848
Staffordshire Advertiser 1 December 1849
Staffordshire Advertiser 2 May 1863
Wolverhampton Chronicle and Staffordshire Advertiser 3

March 1858
Staffordshire Advertiser 29 August 1868
Wolverhampton Chronicle and Staffordshire Advertiser 8 February 1860

Transport
Staffordshire Gazette and County Standard 25 March 1841
Staffordshire Advertiser 1 October 1864
Staffordshire Advertiser 14 May 1864
Staffordshire Advertiser 6 August 1864
Birmingham Daily Post 28 September 1872
Staffordshire Gazette and County Standard 20 June 1840
Lichfield Mercury 24 February 1888
Staffordshire Advertiser 30 April 1864
Lichfield Mercury 25 August 1899
Lichfield Mercury 7 October 1898

Drowning
Staffordshire Advertiser 6 November 1847
Staffordshire Advertiser 16 July 1853
Staffordshire Advertiser 19 January 1861
Staffordshire Advertiser 16 January 1864
Staffordshire Advertiser 14 May 1864
Walsall Advertiser 23 January 1909

Miscellaneous Accidents
Staffordshire Advertiser 4 February 1865
Gloucestershire Chronicle 31 May 1879
Wolverhampton Chronicle and Staffordshire Advertiser 19 July 1848
Wolverhampton Chronicle and Staffordshire Advertiser 12 May 1852

Birmingham Daily Post 25 August 1869
Birmingham Daily Post 16 June 1890

Guns and Poaching
Staffordshire Advertiser 5 March 1842
HO107 Piece number 973 Book number 5A Folio number 25 Page number 12
Morpeth Herald 11 April 1885
Lichfield Mercury 26 March 1886
RG11 Piece number 2781 Folio 9 Page 9
Staffordshire Advertiser 6 January 1866
Staffordshire Advertiser 26 May 1866
Lichfield Mercury 30 November 1888
Lichfield Mercury 22 September 1899
Birmingham Daily Post 1 May 1872

Escapes
Hobart Town Gazette 24 February 1827
Staffordshire Advertiser 26 June 1841
Staffordshire Advertiser 15 February 1845
Lichfield Mercury 30 September 1892
Aris's Birmingham Gazette 15 April 1865
Wolverhampton Chronicle and Staffordshire Advertiser 13 September 1865
Bradford Observer 15 February 1873
Wolverhampton Chronicle and Staffordshire Advertiser 31 August 1859
Lichfield Mercury 18 June 1886
RG11 Piece number 2781 Folio 87 Page 1
RG11 Piece number 2781 Folio 88 Page 4

Chapter 3

Damage
Wolverhampton Chronicle and Staffordshire Advertiser 18 April 1855
Wolverhampton Chronicle and Staffordshire Advertiser 30 December 1857
Wolverhampton Chronicle and Staffordshire Advertiser 3 January 1844

Cruelty
Worcester Journal 11 May 1820
Wolverhampton Chronicle and Staffordshire Advertiser 14 October 1835
Lichfield Mercury 24 May 1895
Lichfield Mercury 4 October 1901
Lichfield Mercury 24 April 1896

Theft & Robbery
Derby Mercury 9 September 1813
Stafford Criminal Records
Derby Mercury 5 June 1817
Birmingham Journal 2 June 1827
Birmingham Journal 15 March 1828
Staffordshire Advertiser 18 July 1829
1841 HO107 Piece number 973 Book number 4 Folio number 13 Page number 19
Reprinted in Illustrated Police News 1 April 1893
Wolverhampton Chronicle and Staffordshire Advertiser 7 March 1832
Stafford Criminal Records
Staffordshire Advertiser 31 March 1838
Staffordshire Advertiser 19 October 1839

Staffordshire Gazette and County Standard 29 April 1841
Wolverhampton Chronicle and Staffordshire Advertiser 14 July 1841
Wolverhampton Chronicle and Staffordshire Advertiser 8 November 1848
Staffordshire Advertiser 28 April 1849
Wolverhampton Chronicle and Staffordshire Advertiser 4 October 1848
Wolverhampton Chronicle and Staffordshire Advertiser 4 July 1849
Staffordshire Advertiser 8 March 1851
Wolverhampton Chronicle and Staffordshire Advertiser 16 April 1851
Wolverhampton Chronicle and Staffordshire Advertiser 15 March 1854
Wolverhampton Chronicle and Staffordshire Advertiser 28 June 1854
Staffordshire Advertiser 20 October 1860
Staffordshire Advertiser 2 July 1864
Staffordshire Advertiser 20 July 1867
Birmingham Daily Gazette 19 October 1865
Staffordshire Advertiser 6 July 1850
Staffordshire Advertiser 8 March 1851
Staffordshire Advertiser 25 August 1866
Lichfield Mercury 23 March 1888
Sheffield Daily Telegraph 10 September 1890
Birmingham Daily Post 9 September 1890
Lichfield Mercury 29 August 1884
Lichfield Mercury 21 November 1884
Lichfield Mercury 9 November 1888
RG12 Piece number 2217 Folio 130 Page 1
RG12 Piece number 2217 Folio 133 Page 7

Lichfield Mercury 19 May 1893
Birmingham Daily Post 25 July 1893
Lichfield Mercury 3 November 1899
Lichfield Mercury 20 February 1914
Lichfield Mercury 1 July 1892
Lichfield Mercury 20 January 1899
Lichfield Mercury 3 June 1904
Wolverhampton Chronicle and Staffordshire Advertiser 12 March 1862
RG09 Piece number 1980 Folio number 17 Page number 6
Lichfield Mercury 21 April 1893
Staffordshire Gazette and County Standard 4 March 1841
Staffordshire Advertiser 23 January 1830

Chapter 4

Staffordshire Advertiser 8 June 1822
Staffordshire Advertiser 23 April 1836
Wolverhampton Chronicle and Staffordshire Advertiser 14 July 1841
Marriages Dec 1842 Birmingham 16 451
HO107 Piece number 1987 Folio 87 Page 10
Sheffield Daily Telegraph 10 March 1857
Eddowes's Journal, and General Advertiser for Shropshire, and the Principality of Wales 3 May 1854
Shrewsbury Chronicle 20 March 1857
RG09 Piece Number 1979 Folio Number 87 Page 1
Wolverhampton Chronicle and Staffordshire Advertiser 25 May 1859
Wolverhampton Chronicle and Staffordshire Advertiser 27 August 1862
Staffordshire Advertiser 2 May 1863

RG10 Piece number 2878 Folio 30 Page 7
Staffordshire Advertiser 6 August 1864
Staffordshire Advertiser 20 July 1867
Birmingham Daily Post 22 June 1871
Lichfield Mercury 8 October 1880
Staffordshire Sentinel and Commercial & General Advertiser 23 October 1880
Lichfield Mercury 29 October 1886
Staffordshire Advertiser 23 June 1849
HO107 Piece number 973 Book number 4 Folio number 40 Page number 4
Staffordshire Sentinel 28 January 1878
Liverpool Mercury 15 April 1880
RG11 Piece number 2781 Folio 42 Page 27
Lichfield Mercury 20 June 1884
Wolverhampton Chronicle and Staffordshire Advertiser 20 March 1833
Wolverhampton Chronicle and Staffordshire Advertiser 22 June 1864
Lichfield Mercury 28 June 1889
RG11 Piece number 2781 Folio 79 Page 2
Lichfield Mercury 25 January 1889
Lichfield Mercury 26 October 1888
Birmingham Daily Post 16 August 1892
Lichfield Mercury 12 April 1895
Wolverhampton Chronicle and Staffordshire Advertiser 25 June 1862
Staffordshire Advertiser 2 August 1862
Staffordshire Advertiser 1 August 1835
HO107 Piece number 973 Book number 5B Folio number 3 Page number 2

Chapter 5

Staffordshire Advertiser 13 January 1855

Angel Inn
Staffordshire Advertiser 12 July 1834
Staffordshire Advertiser 10 November 1838
Wolverhampton Chronicle and Staffordshire Advertiser 15 December 1858
Staffordshire Advertiser 28 November 1863
Wolverhampton Chronicle and Staffordshire Advertiser 9 December 1863

Kings Arms
Aris's Birmingham Gazette 17 February 1772

Malt Shovel
Staffordshire Advertiser 9 February 1850
Wolverhampton Chronicle and Staffordshire Advertiser 23 March 1864
Staffordshire Advertiser 2 April 1864
Staffordshire Advertiser 18 January 1868
Staffordshire Advertiser 1 January 1870
Lichfield Mercury 27 August 1880
Birmingham Daily Post 3 July 1890
Lichfield Mercury 26 August 1892
Lichfield Mercury 2 October 1896
Lichfield Mercury 08 September 1899

Lion Inn
Staffordshire Advertiser 29 January 1842
Wolverhampton Chronicle and Staffordshire Advertiser 22 July 1840

Wolverhampton Chronicle and Staffordshire Advertiser 31 August 1853
RG09 Piece number 1980 Folio number 16 Page number 3
Staffordshire Advertiser 23 July 1842
Wolverhampton Chronicle and Staffordshire Advertiser 29 May 1844
Manchester Courier and Lancashire General Advertiser 21 January 1854
HO107 Piece number 2016 Folio 241 Page 23
Staffordshire Advertiser 16 April 1864
Wolverhampton Chronicle and Staffordshire Advertiser 29 January 1834
Walsall Advertiser 7 October 1911

Fleur-de-Lis
Staffordshire Advertiser 21 November 1795
Staffordshire Advertiser 09 January 1796
Staffordshire Advertiser 8 May 1819
Wolverhampton Chronicle and Staffordshire Advertiser 5 May 1830
Staffordshire Advertiser 9 August 1834

Bridge Inn
Staffordshire Advertiser 11 May 1867
Lichfield Mercury 8 June 1900

Chequered Ball
Wolverhampton Chronicle and Staffordshire Advertiser 12 November 1845
Wolverhampton Chronicle and Staffordshire Advertiser 23 September 1857
Birmingham Daily Post 20 September 1892

Swan Inn
Staffordshire Advertiser 9 May 1835
Horovitz, D. "Brewood" 1992, p233
Wolverhampton Chronicle and Staffordshire Advertiser 8 August 1838
Wolverhampton Chronicle and Staffordshire Advertiser 28 June 1843
HO107 Piece number 973 Book number 4 Folio number 4 Page number 1
Wolverhampton Chronicle and Staffordshire Advertiser 4 June 1845
Wolverhampton Chronicle and Staffordshire Advertiser 25 January 1854
Staffordshire Advertiser 2 October 1847
Wolverhampton Chronicle and Staffordshire Advertiser 28 December 1859
Wolverhampton Chronicle and Staffordshire Advertiser 13 June 1849
Wolverhampton Chronicle and Staffordshire Advertiser 3 July 1850
Staffordshire Advertiser 6 December 1862

Admiral Rodney
Wolverhampton Chronicle and Staffordshire Advertiser 12 May 1841
HO107 Piece number 973 Book number 4 Folio number 24 Page number 4
HO107 Piece number 2016 Folio 267 Page 18
Birmingham Daily Gazette 8 July 1870

Drink
Lichfield Mercury 1 February 1884
Lichfield Mercury 11 April 1884
Lichfield Mercury 17 October 1890
Lichfield Mercury 13 July 1888
Lichfield Mercury 14 December 1888
Lichfield Mercury 18 February 1898
Lichfield Mercury 27 January 1888
RG12 Piece number 2218 Folio 6 Page 5
Lichfield Mercury 2 November 1888
Lichfield Mercury 27 January 1899
Lichfield Mercury 18 October 1889
Lichfield Mercury 29 July 1892
Lichfield Mercury 18 January 1895
Lichfield Mercury 17 October 1890
Lichfield Mercury 29 July 1892
Birmingham Daily Post 24 April 1894
Lichfield Mercury 19 May 1899
Lichfield Mercury 3 November 1899
Lichfield Mercury 7 September 1900
Lichfield Mercury 2 August 1895
Lichfield Mercury 24 April 1896
Lichfield Mercury 6 September 1912

Chapter 6

Shops & Property
Wolverhampton Chronicle and Staffordshire Advertiser 27 August 1862
Wolverhampton Chronicle and Staffordshire Advertiser 17 June 1863
RG09 Piece number 1980 Folio number 30 Page number 7

Birmingham Daily Post 1 August 1865
Lichfield Mercury 4 September 1885
Lichfield Mercury 22 September 1899
Lichfield Mercury 23 March 1888
RG11 Piece number 2781 Folio 87 Page 2
Liverpool Mercury 19 September 1899
Wolverhampton Chronicle and Staffordshire Advertiser 20 February 1850
Wolverhampton Chronicle and Staffordshire Advertiser 18 April 1855
Wolverhampton Chronicle and Staffordshire Advertiser 1 November 1848
Staffordshire Advertiser 27 January 1866
Wolverhampton Chronicle and Staffordshire Advertiser 23 March 1864
Wolverhampton Chronicle and Staffordshire Advertiser 18 March 1857
Wolverhampton Chronicle and Staffordshire Advertiser 18 March 1835
Wolverhampton Chronicle and Staffordshire Advertiser 26 December 1832
Staffordshire Advertiser 6 May 1865
Wolverhampton Chronicle and Staffordshire Advertiser 18 January 1865
Staffordshire Advertiser 6 April 1844
Wolverhampton Chronicle and Staffordshire Advertiser 12 February 1845
Lichfield Mercury 9 November 1883
Birmingham Daily Post 12 November 1891

Workhouse
The Sydney Gazette and New South Wales Advertiser 24 June

1830
HO107 Piece number 2016 Folio 267 Page 19
Wolverhampton Chronicle and Staffordshire Advertiser 19 August 1868
Wolverhampton Chronicle and Staffordshire Advertiser 5 December 1838
Staffordshire Advertiser 22 December 1847
Staffordshire Advertiser 13 March 1841
Staffordshire Advertiser 11 December 1847
Staffordshire Advertiser 19 December 1863
Wolverhampton Chronicle and Staffordshire Advertiser 4 October 1865
Wolverhampton Chronicle and Staffordshire Advertiser 4 January 1865
Staffordshire Advertiser 1 January 1870
Birmingham Daily Post 11 January 1876
Wolverhampton Chronicle and Staffordshire Advertiser 20 January 1847
Stafford Criminal Records
Wolverhampton Chronicle and Staffordshire Advertiser 10 August 1842
Lichfield Mercury 14 August 1885
Lichfield Mercury 18 October 1889
Lichfield Mercury 3 May 1895

Health
Staffordshire Advertiser 22 September 1849
Staffordshire Advertiser 15 May 1858
Gloucester Citizen 4 October 1893
Wolverhampton Chronicle and Staffordshire Advertiser 8 November 1848
Exeter and Plymouth Gazette 19 November 1903

Nottingham Evening Post 18 November 1903
Whitstable Times and Herne Bay Herald 21 November 1903
Lichfield Mercury 26 August 1898
RG12 Piece number 2217 Folio 136 Page 14
Lichfield Mercury 29 June 1888
Lichfield Mercury 4 October 1901
Lichfield Mercury 2 September 1898
Lichfield Mercury 4 August 1899
Lichfield Mercury 8 June 1900
Lichfield Mercury 28 September 1900
Lichfield Mercury 8 December 1911
Staffordshire Advertiser 8 April 1843
HO107 Piece number 973 Book number 4 Folio number 8 Page number 9